A Fair Electoral System

INSURE YOUR DEMOCRACY

"One Man, One Vote - Same Man, Same Vote"

RYAN GEORGE SAUNDERS PERALTO Snr., CD

Editor: Julia Tan
Cover and Book Design: Sanya Dockery

Published by
LMH Publishing Limited
Suite 10, 7 Norman Road
Kingston, C.S.O.
Tel: (876) 938-0005
Fax: (876) 759-8752
Email: lmhbookpublishing@cwjamaica.com

Printed and Bound in USA

ISBN-10: 976-8202-30-0
ISBN-13: 978-976-8202-30-7

Contents

Foreword

The centre-piece of any democracy is the voting system. If the voting system is honest the electorate can express a true position. If not, the decision of the electorate would be perverted. This could misguide the country and create a corrupt government.

The electoral system of Jamaica has been plagued by corruption on a massive scale. When it became unbearable and confidence in the system was being lost, Ryan Peralto took the initiative to propose a far-reaching new system capable of unmistakably identifying voters. The system relied on finger printing all voters and storing the prints. At the time of voting the print of each individual who wishes to vote is captured and used to match against the print of the voter stored in the system. If the match is positive, the voter can proceed to vote.

The Electoral Office of Jamaica accepted the system after refinements at the level of the Electoral Advisory Committee. Since then, it has been used in two pilot areas with great success.

This system can be used in many countries and for many purposes especially when identification of persons and authorization to act are critical to the integrity of the process. For instance, the identification of beneficiaries in a system of welfare distribution is often exposed to impersonation. Immigration and law enforcement are two other areas in which it is important to be able to accurately identify and track the movement of persons. All these could be easily dealt with by an identification system which could not be perverted.

The system designed by Ryan G. Peralto Snr. effectively tackles these problems by providing certainty of identity and can be used to clean up any process which requires accurate identification of individuals.

Our nation owes Ryan Peralto a great deal of gratitude for an initiative which will greatly improve our system of governance. The world at large could benefit tremendously from the teachings and use of this initiative.

The Most Hon. Edward Philip George Seaga P. C., O. N.
A Distinguished Fellow at the University of the West Indies
Former Prime Minister of Jamaica.

Acknowledgements

The presentations by members of the Jamaican Legislature were provided by Mrs. Heather Cooke, Deputy Clerk to the Houses of Parliament, from the minutes of meetings prior to their publication in "HANSARD", which is the historical verbatim record of statements made at meetings of the Senate and the House of Representatives.

Comprehensive research was carried out with the permission of Chairman Professor the Honourable Errol Miller CD, OJ and with the cooperation of the Director Of Elections Mr. A. "Tony" Danville Walker, to ensure that the information quoted are indeed accurate reproductions as maintained in the records of operations of the Electoral Advisory Committee and the Electoral Office of Jamaica. Miss Stacie Wong, secretary to the Electoral Advisory Committee, and Miss Samanthia Grant cooperated with the researchers who carried out the investigations and checked the text to ensure the authenticity and accuracy of the quotations and other data included in this chronicle.

My eldest son Ryan Jnr. advised and guided me to write this story on computer which I was using for the first time without having the benefit of any training in how to operate this equipment. His 14-year-old daughter Briana suggested placards in the design on the front cover.

Mr Danville Davidson who is very experienced in the use of computers and Miss Debra Crossley assisted me in tidying up my recordings on the computer and improving its presentation to make it ready for submission to the publishers.

I hereby express my sincere thanks and appreciation to these persons for their cooperation and assistance and to the others who encouraged me to record for the future the facts about this real life experience.

To you who are about to read this tale, let me say that it is my effort to try to bring into sharp focus the critical importance of preserving what is the most important feature of a truly Democratic society which is the right of each and every adult to choose what they wish to do in respect of all things that affect their quality of life.

Yours Sincerely,

Ryan George Saunders Peralto
Commander of the Order of Distinction

Chapter One

FROM WHENCE I CAME

The marriage of Muriel Veronica Saunders to George Stanislaus Peralto produced three girls Velma, Juliana and Veniece and three boys, Ryan, Neville, and Ronald. I am Ryan George Saunders Peralto their first child who came into this world on the first day of spring 1933. My parents and grandparents are dead.

I was born at 20 Cambridge Street, Franklyn Town, Kingston, Jamaica, and lived there for twenty four years and seven months. This was the home of my mother's parents Mabel Theresa (Ramsey) and her husband Ernest Percival Saunders and their children. My mother Muriel, Aunt Verna who married Byron Coombs, owner of Coombs Meats at Bond Street in downtown Kingston and who in partnership with Mr. Sidney Levy and Mr. Larry Udell, an American, founded Jamaica Broilers Ltd suppliers of the "Best Dressed Chicken". Uncle Arthur, who died when I was around 5 years old, and Aunt Cynthia, who is the only surviving member of that generation is married to Dr. Hugh "Palo" March.

Grandpa Saunders developed cataracts in both eyes and had to retire as foreman pipe fitter to the Kingston and Saint Andrew Water Commission, when I was about six years old. I immediately became his eyes and took him for his exercise walks within the town or to visit friends in Franklyn Town and the adjoining areas of Vineyard Pen, Rollington Pen, Campbell Town, Kingston Gardens, Allman Town, Woodford Park, Browns Town, Passmore Town, Rae Town and Newton Square. We also attended church together as he verbally guided me along the roads to places.

Cricket was his favourite game. From time to time the walkway that led from the double wooden entrance gate up to the house was converted into a cricket pitch. With Grandpa directing we used Temper Lime mixed with water to mark out the batting crease at each end. We then soaked along the middle of the back line of each crease with water and used a stone to drive three pieces of stick into the ground, some one and three-quarter inches apart and twenty-eight inches high to act as the wickets.

Temper Lime was produced by convicts at the Main Prison at Tower Street, Kingston from limestone they were made to quarry from Long Mountain Hill along the Palisadoes Road near to the Rock Fort Mineral Bath. It is normally sprinkled on the earth in the animal pens and used in a mixture with water to paint the stones framing our kitchen garden and flower beds to keep away insects.

We got a ball to play cricket by standing on Paradise Street in Rae Town at the fence of the Bellevue Hospital for the mentally ill and shouting to the inmates that we wanted to buy a ball. We would then be told to throw a penny over the security fence and as we did so, back would come a "madman ball" made with some sand tightly wrapped in a piece of cloth and totally covered with knitted cotton twine.

We used a machete from England, sharpened with a three-cornered Black Diamond file from Canada, to carve out the bat from boughs off our coconut tree or that of a neighbour. Grandpa would position me standing at a crease and show me how to hold the bat and play at the ball which my mother or one of my aunts would bowl towards me from the other end of the pitch. The person at bat must try to hit the ball to the boundary of the playing area or sufficiently away from a person fielding within it, to enable both batters to run and exchange positions at the crease before the ball could be picked up and used to hit a wicket.

He also taught me how to bowl. I was made to stand some paces behind a wicket and hold the ball in one hand with my fingers wrapped firmly but not too tightly around it and let it hang down along my side, then run towards the batting crease. On nearing the crease while both feet are still behind the back line, I would swing that arm in a circular motion over my head and on the way down release the ball, to drop in front of the person at bat, to get it to bounce past them and hit the wicket and so bowl them. If I bend my elbow or wrist and straightened it when releasing the ball, this would be seen as throwing and is against the rules.

A batter would also be given out by an umpire if — they hit the ball in the air and a member of the opposing team on the playfield caught it, or if they miss the ball, and it hit them and not the wicket because they stood in front it, or if they go forward to hit the ball and have both their feet and bat outside the crease and the ball is fielded and used to hit the wicket or as batters try to exchange ends to make a run the ball is used to hit a wicket while one of them or the bat they are holding is not inside the batting crease to which they were going.

Later I learned that this game gave birth to the phrase "that's not cricket", which is used, especially by English people, to describe failure in keeping with an agreement when dealing with matters or with the principles or rules that govern such activities.

The walkway and the land behind the house on which there was the kitchen and a pit toilet, are where we children were also taught to play games like hop-scotch, marble, soccer, skip rope, long jump, chevy-chase and rounders. We played hide and seek everywhere on the property, and in and under the house that stood some two feet off the ground on concrete pillars.

We learned to play "ping- pong" on the dining table when we got tall enough. Cambridge Table Tennis Club was next door and we were often given used balls. Reading books standing on-edge served as our net and thin pieces of board our rackets. Later we made net and rackets from plywood. The ball was definitely the genuine article. How to make and fly different styles of kites was another activity Grandpa Saunders taught us.

The children of our family and others in our neighbourhood had great fun taking part in these activities in a friendly but very competitive spirit.

At the western end of Deanery Road which separates Franklyn Town from Vineyard Pen were five playgrounds for the use of sports teams of business houses. "Clancarthy" for the staff of Nathan's Store, " Hanna Sports Club" for Mr. Edward Hanna's chain of dry goods stores, the "Chinese Athletic Club" for the Chinese community, and behind that "Caxton Park" for the Government Printing Office. These lay side by side on the north side of the road. Across the road from "Clancarthy" were "Issa Park" for the Issa family enterprises and Mr. Alec Durie's "Times Store". There was also the Alpha Boys School playfield.

These locations were used by the employees and families of those business enterprises to play baseball, softball, badminton, cricket, soccer, lawn and table tennis, darts, cards, dominoes, to hold Track meets, and host other activities with family and friends.

The residents of our community, the adjoining areas, and visitors from outside, came to watch or participate in the events that took place in the afternoons and especially on weekends. Then there was the Alpha Boys Band who practised on the stage on their ground. Band Masters, Mr. Simon Tulloch and after he retired Mr. Ruben Delgado, trained many young boys who became outstanding musicians, such as saxophonists Sammy Ishme, "Little G" McNair and "Big G" Gaynair, slide trombonist Don Drummond, and trumpeter Mullo Williams.

Barry Hutchinson, Carlton Wong and his cousin Leslie Fung now deceased, Dr. Lloyd Wright, my brothers Neville, Ronald and I as Franklyn Town teenagers, plus Roy Delgado a son of the Band Master from Passmore Town, Alvin Hoo from Newton Square and Hugh Wong from Mountain View Gardens, both deceased, and later the leader of the popular music band "Byron Lee and the Dragonaires" from Vineyard Pen, all of us had great fun listening to and watching the Alpha Boys Band practice.

Sometimes when a playground was not being used, we were allowed to play games there or fly our kites. On those very special occasions we did not have to worry about guiding our kites from being hitched up in a tree, which was a big risk when we flew them at home. What a beautiful sight, as various shapes and colours of kites danced in the breeze in glistening sunlight, with the bright blue sky and white clouds in the background. I remember, as if it were yesterday, the peals of joyful laughter that filled the air as we played games in our yards, or on those grounds, while our families supervised, assisted, participated, and watched over us.

Grandpa Saunders also taught me how to read and to pronounce words properly. Everyday from age six until he died, I read to him "The Daily Gleaner" newspaper and in the afternoons except on Sundays, the tabloid "The Daily Express". I would spell any word I could not pronounce and he would say the word.

As I got older, he would explain and we would discuss what each article meant and if or how it and other news that came over the radio may affect our family, our friends, our community and our country, especially during the big war.

As a result of Grandpa having to stay home, I got to meet members of his side of the family who came to visit him. A very special cousin of his is Mrs. Marie Saunders who everyone calls "Aunt Mar" who was married to Frank Leon now deceased. At 103 and still active, she is the oldest living family member. What a strong, lovely and loving person this real lady is. Her daughter

Peggy, now deceased, married Bunny Kirkpatrick and had three sons. Gary is in Information Technology, Wayne is a business manager and Kevin an airplane pilot. Her other child Audrey called "Goody" married Ronnie Alford and they live in Norway with daughters Katrina and Sandra. William "Bill" Saunders her nephew, his wife Ann, their daughter Anna Kaye, along with sons William affectionately called "Mike" and Matthew all live here.

My father while he was a salesman of Singer Sewing machines was recruited to serve in the Royal Air Force and went to England in 1943 to fight in World War II. Grandpa put my mother in charge of the family. She ran the home, and paid the mortgage, service bills, and school fees, from her earnings as a seamstress plus Grandpa's stipend of a pension and the monthly remittance sent by the British Home Office from my father. She also made most of the clothes her family and her sisters and their children wore while they were growing up.

Grandma Mabel's main occupation was to care for Grandpa and help to raise the children. Oh what tender love and care she lavished on her husband and on all of us.

When Aunt Verna married Byron Coombs, they went to live on their own but she still helped us at Cambridge Street. We Peralto kids spent many weeks visiting with her family, when they lived opposite the Saint Joseph Hospital on Deanery Road as you go around the bend towards Merrion Road, and later when they moved to their own big upstairs house on some 15 acres of land at 63 Red Hills Road, in the parish of Saint Andrew, Jamaica.

My brothers and I had really enjoyable times with our Coombs cousins. Richard now lives in Belize, his sister Carol "Jimmy" and brother Wayne live in America, sister Pamela "Pam" and brothers Churchill, and Gordon are dead. We spent many summer holidays playing and learning together. We hunted birds with sling shots that Grandpa Saunders taught us to make to fire small stones. When we shot birds, we would clean, wash, salt, and roast them over an open fire, and eat. We also enjoyed the mango, papaya, sweetsop, soursop, guinep, locust ('stinking toe'), red coat, yellow coat and coolie plums that grew in our yards. We had of course, to help take care of the chickens, the animals and the gardens.

Aunt Cynthia like her sisters attended Alpha Girls School, then worked as a clerk in a store and pitched in with financial help. She then went abroad to live with Grandpa's sister, the late Mrs. Lillian Monteverde in New York and married her boyfriend Hugh March, then a dental student. They lived in America, with their second child Celia, wife of Ian Levy, until he graduated. Their only son Ronald Anthony "Tony" was sent as a baby to live with his grandparents Mr. and Mrs. O. J. March at "March Pen", Old Harbour, Saint Catherine, and daughter Donna, wife of Johnny Chuck was also sent home as a baby to live with us, and became a younger Peralto sister and still enjoys a very special place in our family unit. Their last child Althea, who is married to Roy Quallo, was born after they returned home.

The family at Cambridge Street lived frugally but happily. Each day began with porridge made with grated green bananas, oats, cornmeal, sago, or rice, boiled in water with plenty, of cow's milk and sweetened with wet sugar. This was followed by hot tea made with bush leaves or country chocolate boiled in water, with cows milk, wet sugar and a slice or two of bread, often baked in the brick oven in the outside kitchen, and a boiled or fried egg from the hens we raised, or fried pig tripe that had been cleaned, salted, dried, and smoked in the outside kitchen with the red brick chimney on the roof. Our main meals were usually boiled bananas, sweet and Irish potatoes, yam, yam-pees, cocoa, flour dumpling, rice, plus boiled ackee or callaloo with salt fish seasoned with onion, escallion, thyme, tomato, salt and powdered black pepper and fried in oil which we made by boiling dry coconut meat.

Mama and Grandma Mabel did everything to see that we had enough cooked food to sustain us each day. However, when the cow was giving milk, some days we shared the unsold milk with the calf. Daisy, a Jersey cow gave us at best 7 quarts but her daughter, Adelaide, a Jersey/Holstein, that Grandpa gave me when I was born, had grown up to give us 22 quarts in a single day. The sale of cow's milk helped to support the family and pay school fees. For many years now, far more than I care to remember, I no longer drink cow's milk - enough is enough.

Lemonade made with fresh water from the pipe, wet sugar or sugar head, the juice from lime or sour orange fruits from off our trees was usually available. Sometimes we drank these juices with ice, if the truck from the Kingston Ice Factory came and we were in a position to buy ice and keep it wrapped in a jute bag.

Some Saturdays a couple of our family members would go before day-break to the produce markets downtown to buy food stuff but no matter what else we did, that day was dedicated to cleaning house, washing dirty clothes and house linen, playing games, and was very definitely 'soup' day.

Pea soup was our all-time favourite, be it red kidney, gungo, cow, black eye, or split peas, boiled together with flour and cornmeal dumplings, pieces of yam, dasheen cocoa, sweet potato, slices of breadfruit. Beef soup was next in priority then fish soup, both with irish potato, cho cho, carrot, yampee plus the other items normally put in the pea soup, boiled together with cow bones or fish. There was also chopped callaloo boiled with similar ingredients. No matter the type of soup, it was always generously seasoned with, garlic, onion, black pepper, salt, pimento, and home-grown thyme, escallion, a scotch bonnet pepper. Always included were salted pigs tail or salted beef or corned pork. Occasionally on a Saturday we would have steamed fish usually with boiled white rice and fresh vegetables.

Sunday dinner in mid-afternoon was fairly often very special, rice and peas, brown stewed or roasted chicken and sometimes beef, with fresh lettuce, salad tomato, and boiled cabbage, string beans, okra, or callaloo.

Much of the ground produce, vegetables and chicken we ate were grown in our yard or in that of a neighbour. If none of that was available and there was money which was usually just around the beginning of each month, then Mamma or Grandpa's "Mae Mae" would take me or my brother Neville on the bus with our hamper basket to Solas, Coronation, and Chigger Foot markets in downtown Kingston to buy supplies.

Grandpa Saunders made sure that by age four each of us kids started going to school. He made sure we did our home work each afternoon and that Mamma checked it. On Sunday we reviewed the week's work. Before that we were being taught how to read, write, and do sums (add, subtract, multiply, divide numbers). We also were taught to say our prayers thanking our Creator before going to bed each night and first thing each morning as we got awake.

From about eight years old, our daily chores included cleaning our shoes, the animal and chicken pens, the cages of our pets given to us, (pigeons, guinea pigs, rabbits). Monthly routines centred on cleaning the fish tanks with guppies and swordfish. We also fed them twice daily, tended the kitchen garden, the fruit trees, and the flowers, swept up the leaves in the yard and then took a bath, before eating dinner, doing homework then off to bed.

Going to Church on Sunday mornings and Sunday school in the afternoons were not optional activities.

In addition to being educated, we grandchildren were being trained to manage and handle responsibility. Grandpa Saunders taught us certain things that we were expected to follow. **We were instructed to make sure we passed these teachings on to our children**. I was specially instructed as the eldest grandson to prepare me for when my turn came to be responsible for the family. The nuggets of Grandpa Saunders' wisdom is borne out in these four beliefs.

"There is nothing on this earth more important than family.

Always give back to your community to help others to grow and develop.

There is nothing a person decides to do that they cannot do, once they are prepared to spend the time and effort needed to accomplish it.

Honesty is definitely the best and the only policy."

My sister Velma, brothers Neville, Ronald, and I, and our two deceased sisters Juliana and Veniece were very ,very ,close while growing up as children. Very rarely did we have the usual disagreements and fights as some siblings do. Those of us who are alive are still close and we will remain so until "the Big Man upstairs" calls us and we too must depart this life. All Grandpa Saunders' Peralto grandchildren living are still close to each other, and to Aunt Verna's and Aunt Cynthia's children.

The values taught to me at home were at a early age reinforced by what I learned from Mr. Dillon, my first formal teacher, who operated a preparatory school at his home on Archambeau Road, off Lincoln Road in Lawrence Bush.

Archambeau Road was extended a few years later and the extension named O'Hare Road, and the Member of Parliament for Eastern Kingston and Port Royal decided to live there in the constituency that he represented. He became the third Governor General of Independent Jamaica Sir Florizel Augustus Glasspole GCMG, GCVO, CD, ON.

We hunted birds in Lawrence Bush, an under-developed area east of Wellington Street, behind properties on the east side of Somerset Avenue, south of the cow pasture on the Saint Joseph's Hospital property owned by the Roman Catholic Church and operated by nuns and doctors. It included all properties down O'Hare Road and along Lacy Road and Fernandez Avenue up to the back of those with a main entrance and address on Archambeau, Camperdown and Lincoln Roads.

I won an academic scholarship in 1943, and in January 1944 began attending high school at St. Simons' College on East Street above North Street in Kingston.

A year later, Mamma transferred me as a paying student to Saint George's College. I was the second smallest boy at that school. I immediately came under the direct and strong influence of the Roman Catholic priests, of the Order of the Society of Jesus, who managed and taught at that institution, adjacent to the Holy Trinity Cathedral on North Street in Kingston.

Headmaster Walter Ballou S.J., William "Bill" Hannas S.J., Jack Dorsey S.J., Charles "Andy" Oaks S.J., William " Putto Putto" Feeny S.J, and Dennis Cruchley S.J, (the first Jamaican to be appointed Headmaster of that institution). They not only tutored me but developed in me a better understanding of the real purpose of life, by placing emphasis on some fundamental but important things. Most of these had previously been laid out for me by family members, but these men of the cloth reinforced these beliefs:-

Always give thanks to our Creator and have an abiding faith in Him.

Always respect and care for, women, children, and older persons.

Be vigilant and be ever ready to stand up and defend your rights.

At all times have proper regard for the rights of others.

Success is almost always achieved by dedication and hard work.

All men are created equal.

During my first week at Saint George's College, two big boys held me and tried to bounce me on my bottom on the grassed lawn immediately in front of the O'Hare Building, as a part of my initiation. As I was struggling and fighting to prevent this, along came Fr. "Bill" Hannas, Prefect of Discipline, on the way to his office. He called a halt to this effort, and summoned us to his office in turn.

I later learned that the big boys got their just desserts, from "Mr. Tolly" which was a piece of leather horse rein usually applied to the palm of the hand, but occasionally to the posterior of the boy receiving the lashing while in a bent over position with hands on a desk.

Father "Bill" decided I had to learn to defend myself better so that afternoon he began teaching me to box. My relative size did not improve over the years and of necessity I got pretty good at **"the manly art of self defence"** and even made the school boxing team. I remain eternally grateful to Father "Bill" for adding this dimension to my survival kit. It has indeed served me well over the years.

As I look back, it seems I was one of those students who Father "Bill" not only taught English and Latin, but in whom he took a special interest as he obviously monitored my high school career. He encouraged me to participate in all sports and other extra curricula activities and coached me as a debater and actor in stage plays from the thrid form. He also trained me in public speaking for two years immediately before I became Senior Elocution Champion on November 10, 1950.

During the time I spent at that noble institution I was fortunate to be among students chosen to represent my college in various competitions. I enjoyed an excellent social life with the school family and was deputy Head Boy when I was obliged to leave school and start working to help to support my family.

Then there was the Franklyn Town community the majority of whom lived together as one big family. All children in that community were accountable in our behaviour to all adults and were taught to address or refer to them as Miss, Mr, Mrs, or Aunt or Uncle. Then there were the Police Officers who we also were taught to address by Mr. or their rank. I do not recall their being any police women.

I still remember most families, Ramsay, Cardoza, Sang, Dodd, Rose, Bullock, Alexander, Holman, Brennan, Chung, Fung , Quallo, Beek, Lee Sue, Brash, Smith, Chambers , Reid, Teape, Fong, Roach, Wright, McKen, Bartlett, Adams, Elliot, Cann, Thorpe, Jones, Barnett, Kirlew, Byndloss, Francis, Rae, Miller, Griffith, Hall, Dixon, Craddock, Myrie, South, Taylor, Spence, Campbell, Delgado, and more than one family with the same name but who were not directly related, the Browns, Chins, Davidsons, and Wongs. What a "pot pourri", of races, classes, occupations, shapes, and sizes, living together as a harmonious community.

On the day Grandpa Saunders died in 1947, he sent a message in the mid morning to Saint George's College that I should return home. He died just a few minutes before I walked into his bedroom. At age fourteen I was the eldest male of his lineage in the family and was a pallbearer at his funeral. He lies buried in the Catholic cemetery on Lyndhurst Road, Cross Roads, in the Parish of Saint Andrew.

A few months later, Grandma Mabel told a family gathering that, in the future, decisions affecting our family would not be taken without my input. Grandpa Saunders had bequeathed and prepared me for this. My time had come to begin to assume responsibility and take decisions affecting our family. No longer could I just sit beside him during such meetings and listen, as he had me do since I was ten years old. I had taken to heart the principles he espoused, and I hoped and prayed that my Creator would give me the wisdom and the courage to do what was right.

After my dearest Grandfather died significant quality time was spent by my Godfathers, Mr. Winston Meeks CD a very prominent Jamaican businessmen in his time and Mr. Beauclaire Daly, preparing me some more for life. Both are now deceased. The latter was at different times in charge of the Hope and the Constant Spring Water Treatment Plants, that provide drinking water for the homes in Kingston and St. Andrew, and from where we also got our pet fish.

There was also Mr. Consie Walters, a senior Linotype operator at the Gleaner Company and a long time family friend. Mamma told me that he was the one who suggested to her to name me Ryan. He came to live with us a few years after Grandpa died. Some years later he died, with his head resting in my lap as I sat on his bed reading to him from the Holy Bible at his request. Early in 2005 during a casual discussion with Senator Dwight Nelson CD, another graduate of Saint George's College, I learned that my "uncle" Consie was the brother of his mother and, therefore, his uncle by blood.

In 1949 I took and got 9 subjects in the Senior Cambridge Examination set by Cambridge University of London, England. I graduated in December 1950 as Valedictorian of my class, with a Spanish language prize, the Senior Elocution Champion Gold Medal and the Issa Gold Medal.

I was studying to sit the Cambridge University Higher Schools' Examination and hoping to attend a university to become a Medical Surgeon when I had to leave "the University of North Street" at age 17 years and 8 months, and enter the "University of Life" and started working to help to financially support my family. Two of my siblings were also attending high school and three would soon start and school fees had to be paid to ensure a high school education for them.

Fortunately before leaving Saint George's College, I had received additional exposure to a team of great educators and builders of character in young men. I prayed I was ready to face the world bolstered by the training and influence of the outstanding teaching staff of that institution.

Some other Priests of the Order of the Society of Jesus, nearly all Americans, who taught at Saint George's and helped to shape my life were: - Headmasters Leo Butler and Charles MacMullan, John J. Sullivan, Joseph Connors, Phillip Fuchs, Gerald "Jerry" Hennessey, John Blatchford, Joseph Countie, Joseph Fallon, George Nolan, Leo McGovern, Edward "Lefty" Welch, and scholastics Frank Ryan, Francis Shea and John Carol. Jamaican Jesuits among the tutors were the siblings Frs. Charles and Sydney Judah, and Roy B. Campbell and Leslie Russell.

The senior tutor in Mathematics was a Jamaican layman and a Saint George's College old boy, Mr. Adrian "Chaps" Chaplain, who was rated by his peers as the best of his time.

Then there was the Right Reverend Monsignor Gladstone Orlando Wilson, D.C.L., D.Th., D.Ph., C.B.E., perhaps the most educated Jamaican at that time. He was certainly the first native Diocesan priest of Jamaica, and also a St. George's College old boy.

Holder of a triple Doctorate, Monsignor Wilson was fluent in seven languages and spoke another six including Chinese. Twice he was chosen to address Pope Pious X11, head of the Roman Catholic Church and Bishop of Rome. The first time was when he was elected to represent the student body while attending Urbana College in Rome, the University where he earned his Doctorates. He was also elected a house captain, to date the only West Indian to be so honoured. He was also the first black person appointed a Lecturer at that institution and taught there for many years. He became a Catholic priest and while he was attached to the Chancery of Bishop Emmett, the Pope was celebrating fifty years as a priest, and again he was selected to address His Holiness.

We Peralto kids had limited worldly goods to enjoy while growing up, but oh my God what a generous fountain of love and training we enjoyed. Mamma, Grandpa and Grandma Saunders, our aunts Verna, Cynthia and their informally adopted sister Avis who later migrated to live in England, other family members, our friends, our neighbours and our teachers all, they loved, taught, and cared for us. Thank you my God for giving them to us.

Chapter Two

A SYNOPSIS OF MY ADULT LIFE

All the persons mentioned each and every one, played a part in instilling in me values that have guided my life and are a part of my being. These beliefs and commitments have made me whatever I am, despite my own natural failings.

As soon as I left Saint George's College I was invited into membership of the Honour Society of that school, the *"Phi Gamma Chi."* From 1951 to 1965, I was elected annually to the board of the Old Boys Association and served as Secretary from 1958 to 1960. I represented them at cricket, billiards and darts and in the early 60s began playing Bridge. I did not accept nomination to the board of that association in 1966.

Our Old Boys Association operated from a adjoining property north of the school grounds, with entrances also on Melbourne Road, which no longer exists off South Camp Road, and from East Avenue in Kingston Gardens.

A couple years earlier, past students, Allan Wynter, George Desnoes, Abe and Joe Issa, R. E. Taylor, Winston Meeks, A. D. "Gussie" De Leon, F.X. "Pancho" Rankine, Cecil Knight, Lance Drydale decided and with the support of others bought the property on behalf of the old boys and began developing it. Fort Simons, the American military base at Verna Field in the Parish of Clarendon was being shut down and materials were bought from there to build a clubhouse. Wilson Chung, architect and Leonard I. Chang, engineer, Georgians both dead, were appointed to develop the property.

The very active old boys and our Senior and Junior League Soccer teams plus our Senior, Junior, and Carib Cup Cricket teams had our own grounds at last. This took the pressure off using the college for meetings and its play field, " Winchester Park" to host home games and this new playfield was also to be used by the students of the college by arrangement. The facility was named "Emmett Park " in honour of Bishop Thomas Addis Emmet S. J., Vicar Apostolic and Head of the Roman Catholic Church in Jamaica.

I continued as a lead actor on stage as a member of the Caribbean Thespians theatre group, doing at least two plays a year, until I gave it up in 1959 to please my wife. Some of my extra curricula activities just had to go and this became a casualty.

Mamma and Neville went to England to live with my father during the early 1950s. I looked after the family. After the war, my father qualified as a Quantity Surveyor and joined the Peter Lind Company of London, England. One of the projects on which he worked, was the London Post Office, the first public building to be erected anywhere with a revolving top floor.

On November 2, 1957 I married Lorna, daughter of Mr. Vincent Tyrie and his lady wife Lucille, nee Hollar, at Holy Trinity Cathedral, North Street, Kingston. Lorna and brother Colin survive their parents and brother Peter. I was baptised, christened, confirmed, and attended Mass at that church some weekday mornings and on Sundays from about age seven and later taught Sunday school while I lived at Cambridge Street. Almost every priest who taught me at my Alma Mater took part in our wedding ceremony, which was conducted by Monsignor Gladstone Wilson, a classmate and good friend of my father-in-law.

Uncle Byron had sold the Red Hills Road property a couple years earlier and it was sub-divided into house lots. I paid down on a lot two years before I got married. I had my first house built there in 1959, and moved into my own home at 15 Dupont Avenue, Red Hills Gardens, Saint Andrew, in November, with Lorna and Ryan Jnr., my son who was born on October 30, 1958, from a rented bungalow at 24 Dunrobin Avenue, Saint Andrew the home of Mr. John and Mrs. Phyllis McPherson, their daughter Marjorie and son Ian. Mrs. Mac was a teacher at Camperdown High School which Lorna attended before doing a secretarial course at Alpha Academy.

I again moved my family late in 1972, this time with my brood of eight kids to 7 Montgomery Way, Stony Hill. I learned as the third owner of that home that once the government changed, for the first time since Jamaica got Independence on the 6th of August 1962, the second owner decided to leave and migrated to Canada.

What a lovely large home. The upstairs of the main house has four bed-rooms, each with its own bathroom, and a Master Bedroom suite. Downstairs there is a family room, dining room, kitchen with breakfast nook, living room and a front veranda. The view from the Mona Dam, the City of Kingston, the Kingston Harbour and the Docks, the airports, and the town of Port Royal to the south then westward to Edgewater, the Hellshire Hills and Bernard Lodge Sugar Estate and the Blue Mountains to the northeast. The helper's quarter has three rooms, a bathroom, laundry room, and two downstairs storerooms, in a separate building. There was also a swimming pool with wooden deck and below it change rooms, shower, and powder room.

This for my rather large young family was like what we imagined going to Heaven would be. If you grew up in a large family living in a typical size house, you will quickly understand and appreciate how we would enjoy the new large home. Lorna still lives there and so do our children when they visit with their family.

Our eldest daughter Aven Andrienne married Jerry Nichols. They have daughters Arielle and Sarah, and sons Alexander and Matthew Ryan who has my first name by family agreement. Daughter Mishka Jayanne married and divorced and has son Giovanni Luke. We have five sons. Ryan Jr. our eldest child, married Ingrid Forbes and they have a daughter Brianna. Tarn Andru married her sister, Patricia and they have daughters Tian, and Chloe and son Nikhail. Shaun Kristen married Donna Chin and they have daughters, Mayelle, Gabriella, and Nia McKenzie. Dane Firth married Shelly McFarlane. They have daughters Krista and Tamya a cancer patient from age four, and a baby son Dante. Jon Marquis married Victoria Fowler and they have daughter Bailee, and sons Zachary, Gabriel, and Lucas Ray. Jerry and Victoria are Americans; the other in-laws are Jamaicans.

Our fourth child and second daughter Dia Tamya, married, divorced, and died childless in a car accident on January 5, 1998 in Key West, Florida, USA, where she taught school. She had a Masters Degree in Education from Colombia University, New York, USA, and planned to return home to open her own school. Shaun was sent to bring her body home. Stella Maris the Catholic Church on Shortwood Road, Saint Andrew, was full and overflowing for her funeral on January18th.Her body lies in the churchyard at Tom's River, in the hills of the Parish of Saint Andrew.

The outpouring of sympathy by the members of our family, our friends and associates both local and foreign, plus the more than a thousand sympathisers who attended her funeral, was then and still is a source of great comfort to our family.

My family members, particularly the in-laws who Dia Tamya made sure felt welcome into our family, will tell you that her death caused severe pain and left an ache that in my case just will not go away. I hugged her at Tarn's home on Boxing Day as we discussed her coming home. A few days later, she left to spend, the New Year's celebrations with friends in Florida. They have placed a leaf on the "Tree of Life" in the Catholic Church, "Star of the Sea," in Key West in her memory. A cross on the road side marks where she had the car accident in which she died. I will visit them one day. Her friends and colleagues in New York sent a plaque in her memory to Lorna.

My sister Velma moved to Canada shortly after I got married. Except for her, all my siblings married Jamaicans. My brother Neville married Laura White and she and their daughter Tanya and his other children Suzzanne, Pane and Damian live in the USA. My brother Ronald married Eloise Hay and they, their daughters Charmaine and Maria and two sons, Stephen and Bryan and his other daughter Andrea live in Florida, USA. My sister Juliana married Alvin Allenger of Grand Cayman and lived in Jamaica for a few years before moving to Cayman. Both are deceased. Their daughters Shiona and Melody and son Shane live there. My sister Veniece, now dead, married Peter Arnett son of the Honourable Vernon Arnett CD, OJ and his wife Sybil, both deceased. Their son Vernon is dead, daughter Peta Gay lives in Florida, and Peter lives in Toronto, Canada. Velma married Philip Hersom, an Englishman. She has no children and they live in Canada as well.

At the age of 26, I went on a business/holiday trip in 1959 to Europe and paid a surprise visit to my father at his office in London, England. I had not seen him since age ten. We had not corresponded since 1950 because he refused to assist me to go to university in the USA when I was offered a limited scholarship. I spent a week with him, during which I made my peace. "The University of Life" had not treated me too badly and I felt I could afford to forgive him. I certainly remembered "**Always respect your elders**" and after all he was my father. I also visited "aunt" Avis, then Mrs. Williams, and her husband and daughter Rita who lived in London.

My father visited with us in Jamaica three times afterwards before he died in 1996 and left us a villa on the Costa Bravo in Spain, the land of his lineage. My sister Velma and I attended his funeral in England.

Grandma Mabel and Mamma lived in Edgewater, St. Catherine, Jamaica, after I arranged for their removal from Franklyn Town in 1972. Early one morning on her way back from the kitchen where she had gone well before daylight to make her usual cup of coffee, just as she had been doing from ever since I can remember, Grandma fell and broke the thigh bone in her right leg.

While she was recuperating in hospital, I was told that she had been put on pills to avoid her developing a blood clot. After one of my daily visits I left her late one evening in good spirits and went home to my family.

At about 6.30 a. m the following morning I was telephoned and told that she had died earlier that morning, apparently from a heart attack caused by a blood clot. I immediately went to the hospital and while there observed that she had not been given the pills and became very angry. I discussed this with my uncle-in-law, Dr. Hugh March, and he persuaded me not to pursue it. She died at the age of 88 in 1977.

In 2002 my dearest Mamma while visiting with me sustained a broken pelvis and hip, when she fell on the concrete tile floor in my living room in my home in Barbican, Saint Andrew, Jamaica. She was demonstrating to me how my 3 plus year old daughter Ronella danced for her.

She remained in Jamaica for over a year recuperating before returning overseas, but she was never the same again. I visited her in Toronto, Canada, in September 2004, and she died the following month at age 94 on November 26. I returned to attend her funeral along with all our other family and some friends who live abroad.

She had spent most of her life overseas since the middle of the1970s away from our Jamaican trauma, but continued to exercise her influence over the entire family, as our Matriarch. My sister Velma, as agreed, brought her ashes home in January 2005 and family members and friends who live in Jamaica attended a Memorial Service at the Stella Maris Catholic Church to pay their last respects as others of them who live overseas had done in Canada.

I knew that Grandma Mabel was born in eastern Saint Thomas, Jamaica. However, I never met any of her family. Mamma was recuperating in a nursing home after her fall. I went as usual to visit her one evening when a nurse told me that she seems to have found a new family member earlier that afternoon. As a elderly man walked by Mamma in the recreation room, she called out "Hello sonny, come here". He hauled himself to his full height supported by a walking stick and looking somewhat perturbed came to her. " My name is Muriel Peralto" she continued "and you remind me of my grandfather. What is your name?". His countenance softened as he replied. "My name is Carol Ramsey", whereupon she very quickly added "My grandfather was a Ramsey. What was your grandfather's first name and did he have a brother" and so they continued.

I then went to her room and she repeated the story adding that after swapping notes they established that their grandfathers were brothers but the grandchildren had never met. She was obviously very delighted at discovering a cousin. I told her that I had known attorney-at-law Mr. Carol Ramsey, since 1977.

I later visited Mr. Ramsey and his wife who lived with him in the nursing home. We discussed family connections and agreed we were relatives. Some weeks later Ryan Jnr. and I were invited home by his son Robert and his wife Sandra, sister of Ian Levy, all of whom we knew before, to meet with the Carol Ramsey family unit . Since then, Robert and I have made a point of seeing each other regularly and have been explaining our relationship to other family, members in Jamaica and abroad and also our friends. Mrs. Carol Ramsey died in 2005 and I attended the funeral service. Mr. Carol Ramsey died on February 11, 2006. Ryan Jnr., Lorna and I went to his funeral and I spent the afternoon with five of his six children and other family members and their close friends who were there.

My siblings and cousins, following in the footsteps of our mothers are all committed and adhere to our family traditions. We are very aware of our responsibility and obligation to our immediate family unit but we are in no doubt about our responsibility to the wider family. Every family member must be made to understand that we are all very important to each other and integral to the future of our family as a whole. Most of our spouses, our offspring and their lovely partners, have learned to understand and respect our very special family relationships, but some in-laws and their family members find it quite difficult to accept and conform to these expectations.

Many of our children attended universities abroad in societies where much emphasis is placed on individuality, self reliance and independence at the expense of almost everything else.

Some spouses have had similar experiences and so they and their children find it difficult to fully embrace our family traditions. They are apparently not comfortable with this special bond we share, and our heritage imposed obligation to each other which is inherent in our family lineage.

Our family traditions must never be forsaken or compromised. Our bloodline, and those who marry into it and thereby become a part of shaping its future, must remain forever committed and bonded to each other through thick and thin. This is the way of our family.

What a pity the drive to succeed, and the shortage of opportunity at home have driven so many Jamaicans including family members to live abroad. I am sorry Grandpa Saunders, I have been trying desperately to help to build a better Jamaica and I will die trying. One day, one day, it will happen and some of your seed will be numbered among those who like you, tried to make it so.

My brother Neville, his son Neville Jnr. with his wife Karla and daughter Catherine, my half sister Mrs. Lorna McFarlane (Peralto) her sons Ian, Stokley and Raul, two of my sons Ryan Jnr., and Tarn Andru with their families, their mother and my life long friend, Lorna from whom I have been long separated, plus my six year old daughter Ronella, her mother Maureen Scott and I live in Jamaica.

Working to help to make the land of my birth a place in which people are happy to live, especially our family members, has occupied most of my adult life to date. That is why I became directly involved in the politics of my country and remained so for twenty five years.

Most of those years were spent in the political main stream. I served in the Jamaican Parliament, as a Senator from 1980 to 1983, a member of the House of Representatives 1983 to 1989 and again as Senator from 1990 to 2002. Incidentally, Senators are not paid a salary.

In 1986 I was appointed Minister of State in the Ministry of National Security and was transferred a few months later to the Ministry of Foreign Affairs, Trade and Industry with responsibility for Trade and Industry. Immediately I agreed to the transfer, I removed myself from my operating businesses. In 1989, after I and my party lost that election, I took the opportunity to reduce my political activities for a year while I concentrated on seeing to it that two of my companies operated to satisfy large debts they had developed and then shut them down permanently.

My experience from being directly involved in the politics of my country for a quarter of a century will be the subject of another chronicle.

Chapter Three

WHY POLITICS?

At the age of 33 I had worked for over fifteen years with my first and only full time employer. We had a major disagreement three years earlier over share holding in NACO Caribbean Limited that I persuaded the Australian firm to change their position and establish locally. In 1963 I formed Modern Partitions Limited to make and install aluminium framed Demountable Office Partitions for the first in Jamaica. In 1966 I again had a serious disagreement with my Managing Director, this time over company development policy. I resigned, acquired my employers' shares in MPL and concentrated as Managing Director and majority shareholder on developing that company and because the first of my lineage in Jamaica to operate their own company. I agreed verbally with the owner not to make products to compete with his companies and I never did. A few years later time he closed the local company. I still own shares in the parent company.

Nine years and two more businesses later, I and my family became concerned that democracy in Jamaica was under serious threat. The governing party, the People's National Party, was busy promoting Socialism as the preferred system of government.

Lorna's brother Peter, who has gone to university in Canada and was by then a Canadian citizen, petitioned and got permission from the Canadian government for my family to migrate there. As requested, Lorna and I visited their Embassy, discussed the matter, and thanked them. I was not prepared to leave my country.

In 1977 I felt compelled and obliged to join the Jamaica Labour Party, the political opposition. I could no longer stand by and

watch my country become a Communist State. I had visited some of those in my travels and I decided I had to get involved to help to prevent this happening to my country no matter what it may cost me. No way, not my Jamaica, not in my lifetime would this country turn Communist.

I then dedicated twenty five years of my life working, for a political party I had determined from some years earlier, offered the type of visionary leadership my country needed then, and needs today.

Prior to this and after leaving school I had volunteered a great deal of my time to Community Development. I served the Saint George's College Old Boys Association, then became a Jaycee in 1964, treasurer of the Kingston Boys Scouts 1966, Chairman –" Nuggets for the Needy 1967"- a Kingston Jaycees/Jamaica Broadcasting Corporatin Charity Fund Raising Project and I expanded it island-wide. Elected President of Kingston Jaycees 1968, I was made a JCI Senator in 1969 and awarded Life Membership in Junior Chamber International. I was appointed Chairman, National Volunteers, Kingston Chapter for 1969 and elected President of Jamaica Junior Chamber-1970, then elected to the Board of the Jamaica Manufacturers Association from 1971 to 1979 serving for three years as Vice President. I was also elected in 1977 to the Board of the Caribbean Association of Industry and Commerce and appointed on the Student Placement Board of the University College of the West Indies.

My family attended Holy Mass together every Sunday except for illness or overseas travel, to give thanks and praise to our God for being so kind and watchful over us. I was leading a busy but settled life helping to raise a family and build a better homeland.

In 1977 I became convinced our democracy was definitely at immediate risk because of the philosophy and policy direction being pursued by the incumbent Prime Minister in his approach to governing my country. My life was about to undergo a dramatic change.

In 1980, I returned and again began taking a keen interest and really getting involved in the welfare and life of the residents of Central Kingston which was represented by the Prime Minister. The entire character and quality of life had changed dramatically for the worst, in the community where I was born and raised. Most families that I knew no longer lived there.

Some residents of Southside, an area in the capital city, and by then one of the most impoverished and destitute communities in the country, chased their Member of Parliament from the area one Sunday morning and sent for me. I went there the following morning and became their parliamentary candidate. **I had become a political activist, something that previously held no attraction for me**.

Then on 19 April 1980, the Daily Gleaner carried the report on what it labelled the "**Gold Street Massacre**" that was visited on those people. The night before men came into the area and opened fire on residents attending a community dance. Five bullet-riddled bodies were left behind.

Parliamentary Elections took place 30 October 1980, and I got my first exposure to voting day mal-practices which enlightened me that such behaviour often determined the result of an election. Based on this experience, I concluded that the Jamaican electoral system was in urgent and desperate need of reform.

Lack of a secure and accurate identification system allows incorrect and improper identification of electors and permits impersonation and fraudulent voting. Access to unused ballot papers allows illegal voting. Access to ballot papers marked by electors allows persons to spoil or remove good votes which cannot then be counted.

I was persuaded to the view that the absolute reliance on persons to operate and manage the process and guarantee its integrity , which is the basis on which the Jamaican electoral system is structured and depends entirely, is by far the major factor that allows such abuses of the system to be committed.

THE ABUSES BEING COMMITTED AGAINST THE JAMAICAN ELECTORAL SYSTEM CONSTITUTE A DEFAMATION OF THE INTEGRITY OF THIS PROCESS AND WERE AND STILL ARE MAJOR THREATS TO THE PRESERVATION OF DEMOCRACY IN THE BELOVED LAND OF MY BIRTH.

I have always and will always have an abiding commitment to become personally involved and do anything that lies within my power to protect Jamaica and our people , once I am satisfied that they are threatened.

My travels to numerous countries since the mid-1950s has served to strengthen and reinforce this commitment. The freedoms that I have been accustomed to enjoy in my beloved Jamaica have never been replicated in the many countries I have visited during the fifty-five years that I have been going overseas.

I had heard over the years, from persons I thought reliable, that our election process had been manipulated in indvidual constituencies. Being politically naive I really did not believe this. **The abuses so angered me it spawned a total rejection of such practices and gave birth to the idea of taking steps to prevent such behaviour. My sense of fair play was assaulted and I was moved to act to protect my rights as well as the rights of my countrymen.**

I was determined that I had to find a method to protect our Constitutional Rights to vote to elect by the genuine choice of the majority of registered voters, the persons from among us who, we, as a people, would choose to govern our nation.

Jamaica's electoral system just had to be improved. Very soon it became crystal clear that so long as the system has to depend on the exercise of human discretion for its integrity, this may be impossible to achieve in a society where so many are under-educated, poor, and vulnerable. In fact, the integrity of the electoral results will remain at an unacceptable level of risk, for as long as humans remain in direct and total control of the process by which others exercise their right to vote.

I recognized that to accomplish this, I would have to design a automated system capable of performing a number of different functions:-

1   Process the information on persons who apply to be listed as voters to develop an accurate record of all Registered Electors on which each person appears once only.

2 Use this accurate record of Registered Electors to print the voters list.

3 Use the data on file in an automated process to identify each elector on voting day before allowing them to cast a vote .

4 Allow electors it identifies to vote once only.

5 Post each vote cast to the account of the candidate chosen.

6 Maintain a record of the electors permitted to vote, and who voted.

7 Safeguard transaction records from being changed, spoilt or removed.

8 Count the votes cast for each candidate after the poll closes.

9 Print out a tally sheet of the count of the votes.

10 Print out a list of the names of the electors who voted.

Automated electronic systems existed that allowed choosing a candidate and recording and counting the votes. None existed that could accurately identify electors before permitting them to vote, or could guarantee restricting voting to registered electors and restricting each elector to vote once only.

In a discussion with party officers, Party Leader the Honourable Edward Seaga, made the point that counting the votes was not the crux of our local election problem .What Jamaica needed was a system that could guarantee " One man, One vote---Same man, Same vote".

Chapter Four

JAMAICA'S ELECTORAL SYSTEM IN TROUBLE

The Representation of the People Act which governs how Jamaican National Elections are to be conducted provides that certain conditions shall be maintained in order that voting can be properly carried out, as summarised below.

1. **Anyone 18 years old and over who is a Jamaican citizen, or is a British Commonwealth citizen, and has lived on the island for at least six months prior to the holding of an election, is entitled to be registered as an elector. However, they must apply to have their name and address put on the Voters List for the Polling Division in the Constituency where they live. The List of Voters must be published so that everyone can know which of the residents in each geographic election area are entitled to vote to elect a person as the political representative for that area. Anyone whose name is on the voters' list can become a candidate and contest to be elected to office.**

Problems:-

a) The same person is listed in more than one Polling Division or Constituency, and votes more than once in the same election.

b) The names of persons qualified to be registered as electors and who applied to be listed as voters , are accidentally or deliberately left off the Voters List and so they are not allowed to vote on election day.

c) Electors names appear on the Voters List for a Polling Division other than the one for the area in which they live and expect to vote. On voting day they cannot find out where to vote although they have a voter Identification Card.

d) The names of persons who have migrated or have died remain on the Voters List, and others vote in their name.

2. **Persons whose names are on the Voters List, must be properly identified by the Presiding Officer in charge of the voting process when they visit the Polling Station to vote, and before they are given a Ballot Paper on which are printed the names of the candidate. Each elector should then go to a voting booth and in private mark an X beside the name of the person they choose, fold the Ballot so that no one can see who they chose, and bring that vote back to the Presiding Officer. The Presiding Officer is to remove the perforated tab on which is pre-printed the number of that Ballot Paper and, after that elector has dipped their right index finger in the voting ink to show that they have voted, place that Vote in the Ballot Box.**

Problems:-

a) Improper identification, be it deliberate or accidental, allows persons to vote in the name of others.

b) Some bona fide electors whose names are on the Voters List are denied identification and not allowed to vote.

c) Electors are not required to dip their finger in the voters ink and so they can return and are allowed to vote again.

3. **Ballot papers must be kept safe and only marked by electors to cast their vote, after which they must also be kept safe and then be accurately counted for each candidate after the close of the poll.**

Problems:-

a) Access to official Ballot Papers allows incorrect persons to mark some of these for a particular candidate and have them counted as legal votes.

b) Access to unmarked Ballot Papers allows someone to obtain a Ballot Paper and mark it for a particular candidate. It is then given to an elector who conceals it and takes it into the voting booth and substitutes it for the official ballot issued to them and has it dropped into the ballot box to be counted as their vote. That elector then leaves the voting station with the unmarked officially issued Ballot Paper and exchanges it for the previously agreed compensation and that procedure is repeated as often as there are electors willing to sell their vote.

c) Access to Ballot Boxes allows persons to spoil or steal properly marked Ballot Papers, which are then not counted as valid votes.

4. Electors must be allowed to vote in private and in conditions that are "free and fair, and free from fear."

Problems:-

a) Crowds gather at Polling Station locations and intimidate electors into casting their vote for a particular candidate.

b) Electors are threatened by partisan supporters to vote for a particular candidate and are required to show how they marked their ballot paper to some one to satisfy them that the elector had voted as they were threatened to do.

Developing a system to prevent illegal voting

In 1986 I was again exposed to abuses of the Jamaican voting system. I was by then General Secretary of the Jamaica Labour Party. The first hand reports from key party organizers across the island on the conduct of that election enabled me to assess the full impact of those abuses on the results of that contest, on an island-wide basis. It seemed that the corrupt methods least likely to raise alarm among those electors were selected and used across the country, in order to mask the massive assault on the system. However, if confrontation developed, so be it.

The voting day strategies employed in the 1986 Jamaican Parish Council Elections, appeared to have made ample use of all the known methods of manipulating the process. The extent of this assault on the system had never before been experienced according to long serving political activists, who considered such activity merely as an increase in the degree of "ginalship" that had been practised over many years. They were disappointed and upset at losing but for the most part they merely took it as being extremely rough political gymnastics, much to my surprise and disgust.

I concluded that this dangerous and despicable 'disease' that infected the election process had expanded over the entire island and was no longer confined to urban enclaves, which my previous exposure to it had suggested.

This new situation forced me to recognize that there really was a very urgent need for the design of a system to prevent such abuses of the process. It compelled me to move with dispatch to complete the development of my system.

After a few more months, I was confident that I had conceived and designed the system that was needed. I was satisfied that the system I had come up with could do the job, to accurately record each elector, print a list of qualified electors with proper address, identify those persons on voting day, permit only them to vote once, record and count their votes, and print out, after the close of the voting, a list of the names of all persons who voted and a tally sheet of the votes cast.

As I reflect on what was visited on the voting process on 29 July 1986, it occurs to me that the nation is still suffering from the aftermath of the residual negative impact of the government led social revolution which was being not so gently imposed, partic- ularly between 1976 to 1980, as the Peoples National Party the incumpent government sought to be re-elected to office with a mandate to change our style of governance. Their stated pur- pose was to install Socialism with Government controlling and operating "the commanding heights of the economy".

The intense and explosive debate that ensued during those years, involved and engulfed just about our entire population inclusive of the Church. As a people, we were being courted by our leaders, Political, Civic, and Religious, to make a choice between Scientific Socialism and what was referred to as the Market Economy or Capitalism.

All of us got very involved in debating the strengths and weaknesses of these systems. The conflicting views spawned on a national scale a pattern of anti-social behaviour never before experienced in Independent Jamaica and became volatile, as our political parties aggressively promoted opposing views. Many of our people became intoxicated with the emotive and inflammatory rhetoric being used by Prime Minister Micheal Manley, who was supported in this debate by a very vocal cadre of his party people, who had fairly recently emerged, and some local university students aspiring to gain recognition as national leaders.

Some of our people influenced by this profusion of verbiage were motivated to pursue an agenda that sought to impose their political persuasion on others to the extent of using force, within as well as against whole communities, to control and suppress views.

The spawning in the mid-1970s of unnecessarily intense and physically aggressive anti-social conduct caused us to be extremely vicious to each other. Too many of us abandoned our traditional persona of respect and civility to each other, to the extent that often times during those years we exhibited little or no regard for the property, and sometimes the life, of our fellow Jamaicans.

This crass and uncivilised behaviour now seeks again to establish itself as a part of our culture. If this distortion is not arrested, expunged, and rejected very quickly, it will consume and destroy us as a people. It is regrettable that we did not anticipate that this offensive behaviour would remain as a feature of our inter-personal relationships especially among the masses of our people up to the present time.

In order to develop this system, I was forced to learn about technologies and equipment that were unfamiliar to me by training, by exposure to, or by experience with their use. This appeared to be my only hope to succeed in developing a system to avoid and prevent the electoral process from continuing to be subjected to abuse and exploitation by the corrupt methods I had identified.

Between 1981 and 1986, I had carried out an international search (UK, USA, France, Germany) to find and familiarize myself with technologies and equipment that had been developed, and were sufficiently mature, to qualify them for consideration, to be used to build a system that could act in the place of humans and carry out the procedures which I had decided needed to be automated.

Very early into my research, I learned that technology existed that could be adopted and adapted to carry out each of these functions. I was also to learn that some of the technologies that initially appeared to be ideally suited to carry out particular procedures were in varying stages of maturity in their development.

This excursion into exploring and trying to really understand the technologies and the equipment, provided me with a kind of mental exercise that I had not experienced or enjoyed for many a year. It opened up my mind to savour a renewed stimulation in mental gymnastics, as I discovered the wonders of the new advances, and wrestled to decide on which was the best suited to carry out each process. Once I was convinced that they could satisfactorily carry out a required process, I had to then learn if, and how, they could be put together to build a composite automated system.

A typical voting station in Jamaica. (photograph by The Gleaner Company Ltd.)

Chapter Five

THE INVENTION

This invention calls for the integration, and synchronization, of technology and equipment, to create a system which captures, stores and processes, biometric and other information as a record of persons. The equipment is then programmed to permit persons whose information is on file, to access and use it to carry out specific functions, after it identifies them. Other end users can access the data stored in the files of the equipment on a limited read-only basis.

Anyone wishing to access the system in order to carry out any activity it is programmed to perform, must first allow the equipment to capture their biometric data equivalent to that on file. The system then processes the new information and goes through the cross-matching sequence against the information on file. If a match is made, the system will permit the person to operate it. If no match is made access will be limited to a read-only basis. No end user is permitted to alter in any way any part of the original data on the system or in its activity records.

The system maintains a complete record of accesses to its files, the persons permitted to carry out activities, the activities carried out, and the date and time such activities were carried out. It can produce print outs of all information in its original file records, its activity records, and a list of the names of everyone it authorized to carry out functions, and the functions they carried out.

Because this system is able to maintain a database of information on selected persons and after identifying them to permit them to carry out specific functions, it eliminates the need for any individual to certify the identity of those persons and give permission for them to be able to use the system to carry out the functions it is programmed to allow them to carry out.

The teachings of my invention can be used to build an electoral system configured to **protect the right of every adult citizen to vote and help to preserve democracy by** insuring that :-

1. Each elector is placed on the voters' list, once only.

2. Each elector is accurately identified by the equipment before they are allowed to vote and vote once only in any election.

3. Anyone not identified by the equipment as a registered voter, will not be allowed by it to vote.

4. The equipment maintains a record of all electors who voted. Immediately an elector has voted their vote is automatically credited by the equipment to the account of the candidate selected by that elector.

5. A print out of all electors who voted can be produced, after the poll closes.

6. A print out of a tally sheet accounting for all votes cast, showing total number polled by each candidate, can be produced after the poll closes.

7. The record of functions carried out by an elector cannot be changed, but an elector is allowed to change the candidate selected prior to voting.

8. All transactions carried out on voting day are automatically transmitted to another location and stored to ensure that a duplicate record of all votes cast is available, if needed, to produce an accurate final count, as well as to secure a duplicate record of all activities carried out by persons using the equipment.

9. Any elector could be allowed to cast his/her vote at any polling station in any place on the island, where they feel secure and comfortable, to exercise their democratic right to vote for the candidate of their choice once the system is configured to access the entire Voters List. A record of that vote will then be automatically transferred

to a voting station where they are listed as an elector. **This will assist greatly to curtail the effect of intimidation.**

NB. **It is impossible to quantify the effect of intimidation on election results:-**

a) **Some electors vote as instructed for fear of being victimised, brutalized and even killed.**

b) **Some electors do not bother to vote because they do not wish to have to disclose how they voted.**

The ability of my system to electronically capture Biometric Elements and other personal information from individuals who wish to use the system, and cross-match it against the information in the system file to identify them before approving use of the equipment to carry out programmed and authorized functions, are most critical features of its design. The fact that it will keep a complete record of all activities and the persons who carried them out, should also act as major deterrent to persons who may be tempted to use the system and still persist in trying to distort the process.

I now wish to record my appreciation for the steadfast support of my children old enough to appreciate how I felt, and what I intended to do. I also wish to thank all of them for the unqualified assistance they consistently and unhesitatingly gave me. Their effort and especially their confidence in my ability to accomplish my objective , a position not shared by most persons who knew of my resolve, contributed significantly to my being kept motivated to work at accomplishing the development of a fool-proof system to identify individuals, guard against impersonation, and prevent corrupt manipulation of processes and systems.

In 1983 as I contemplated on the mechanical design of the system, my third son Shaun who later graduated from New York Institute of Technology as a Computer Engineer carefully instructed me on the capabilities of the computer.

It became obvious that the computer was best suited to be the base on which all the other technologies should be grafted. I, therefore, consulted with my sons Ryan Jr., a industrial engineer of the University of Florida, and Tarn, an architect of New York Institute of Technology, as both had received training in the use of computers.

Those two sons impressed on me the critical importance of the methods used to capture and store each piece of information to ensure good quality data. This would have a direct impact on the design of the computer programmes required to facilitate electronic storage and processing of the information namely, Biometrics, Photographs and Text.

It would also have an impact on the programmes to permit access to the processed data, and allow the manipulation of that data to establish individual identity, and then those programmes to permit persons identified by the system to carry out limited functions, as authorised by the system, and finally, those programmes to integrate the functions of the various pieces of equipment. Thereafter, the equipment and methods to be used to carry out capture, storage and processing of data became a major focus of my research.

My two older daughters, Aven and Dia Tamya, while attending tertiary institutions in the U.S.A, would send me science and technology magazines and publications to assist my search for companies who could provide elements to build the system. Those of my children who attended school in America did so as paying students.

I have had very good reason to be ever mindful of the Biblical injunction that goes "out of the mouth of babes and suckling etc, etc."

Chapter Six

THE INVENTION TO CONDUCT ELECTIONS

While doing my research, Prime Minister Edward Seaga, who was made aware by me of my resolve to stop the abuses of the voting process, invited me after the Parish Council Elections in 1986 to explain my concept to colleagues in a Standing Committee meeting of the party leadership. **This I did**.

I was informed by a couple of persons at the meeting that the Electoral Advisory Committee members had agreed some years before, that if they could match and process fingerprints, this could be used to prevent multiple listing of electors, and greatly assist in the production of a clean and accurate Voters List. To this end the EAC had arranged for the Registration of Electors to include capturing fingerprints. However, they were unable to use the prints as no mechanical process existed to store fingerprints and allow easy and ready access as well as to carry out efficient and fast cross matching in order to quickly sort out the identity of individuals.

After a discussion on my detailed presentation a colleague, who later became a staunch supporter, commented that my concept was reminiscent of "Star Wars". I also recall the support given for the idea at the time by a few colleagues in the leadership team at the party meeting, Errol Anderson, Ed Bartlett, Derrick Smith, Brascoe Lee, Douglas Vaz and Oswald Harding.

Perhaps my failure to get substantial support for my concept from the persons who attended that meeting was because this thinking originated and was being presented by someone who many at the table considered to be a political neophyte, a newcomer, a "fresh foot". Some actually said so.

Whatever the reason was, the vast majority of those in attendance rejected my thinking as being impractical and definitely a futuristic dream. Their reaction was so disappointing and disgusting that it almost made me decide to step away from politics.

I was very upset by the lack of appreciation and minimal concern shown by some persons for what I considered to be a serious threat to our Democracy posed by the abuses of our electoral process. I considered the willingness of persons to ignore these distortions of the system that we use to elect our political leaders, as being worst than the abuses themselves.

Once elected General Secretary of the party in 1985 I began attending party office daily like a paid employee. After that meeting, for months I only went to party headquarters to collect b mail and attend official meetings and operated from my company office and where I continued my research. Then Deputy Chairman, Errol Derrick and Brascoe visited my home on request with a couple of computer people to discuss my idea in detail.

By the middle of 1987 I had settled on the types of technologies that should be employed to build a system that could deal with the problems. I began making direct contact with some overseas producers and users of different types of electronic equipment, that employed the use of these technologies, in order to really understand how they functioned to carry out their particular capability.

This was vital, as I would need to make definite choices to determine which of these could be expected to work well together, and what would be the best approach to integrating the various elements, so that they would function harmoniously as components of a seamless operating system.

Shortly thereafter my colleague, who had made the remark about "Star Wars" but who never the less was keeping abreast of my progress in this regard, namely Prime Minister Seaga, began to give me support and from then on has been unwavering in that position. In fact, implementation of this system became an agenda item at meetings between the leadership of both our major political parties between 1990 and 2003.

One of the things Prime Minister Seaga said to me, on an occasion when we were discussing my concept in depth, was that my proposal if it proved to be feasible could solve the problems of our electoral system, and then he graciously added the comment:- **"this system would be one of the greatest contributions to be made towards the preservation of our democracy since our country became an Independent Nation".**

Over the years, reflecting on that particular comment has often re-energized my efforts, when my learning curve took its toll and my enthusiasm started to wane and falter but most especially since I have been seeking to have the system implemented in an effort to assist to preserve democracy in Jamaica.

Shortly after the March 6, 1990 Parish Council Elections, Party Leader Edward Seaga enquired how far I had reached in developing my concept. I advised that I had settled on how, and what, should be used to build the system and I was satisfied that it was eminently practical to do so. I was still engaged, however, in trying to identify the most competent suppliers of the component elements. I explained that my responsibilities as a Minister of State from 1986 had restricted the time I could afford to spend investigating this, especially between 1987 and early 1989, when I was responsible for Trade and Industry

He asked me if I would make my system available **"free of charge"** to address the weaknesses in Jamaica's electoral system. I answered in the affirmative. In March 1990 he asked me to serve on the Electoral Advisory Committee and offer my system for use and to pursue it being implemented. I agreed. He then made arrangements for me to go to Germany as I wished to visit companies there and France that were reputed to have technologies of interest.

The matter of fairness in the conduct of Elections in many countries of the world was a very current international media topic when Mr. Butros Butro Ghalli, the Secretary General of the United Nations between 1992 and 1996, paid a visit to Jamaica. The Honourable Edward Seaga invited me to accompany him to a meeting with this visitor at the Pegasus Hotel to enable me to have an opportunity to explain my concept to this international official. **This I did**.

Mr. Ghalli was very impressed and said he was unaware that such a system existed and he would very much like to see the system demonstrated. Mr Seaga explained that this was a concept designed by me to address abuses of the electoral system and he thought that the development of this system was something the United Nations should become involved in, and sponsor, in order to put itself in a position to make the system available worldwide to conduct elections.

The Secretary General of the United Nations responded that it was an interesting concept and when developed could prove useful, but it was not the kind of thing the United Nations would get involved in sponsoring.

Chapter Seven

JAMAICA'S ELECTORAL ADVISORY COMMITTEE

This was the first committee of its type established in any country and was as a direct result of the strong, consistent and often belligerent protests of the Leader of the Jamaica Labour Party, the Honourable Edward Phillip George Seaga, MP for Kingston Western.

What I am about to write is partly based on what I read, what was told to me by individuals, and information from the records on the period between 1977 and 1979, since I was not yet directly involved in political activities.

The stridency of the campaign waged by the Honourable Seaga to liberate the management of the electoral process from being under the direct influence, and control of the incumbent government finally came to a head in 1978.

A Parish Council by-election took place in the Parish of St. Mary that was contested by both major political parties. During this campaign some of the resources of the state were generously employed to manage, conduct, and support the candidate of the People's National Party which formed the government.

Shortly thereafter, another by-election was to be held, to fill a seat for Kingston Eastern on the Parish Council of Kingston and St. Andrew. The Honourable Edward Seaga, Leader of the Jamaica Labour Party, advised the Hon. Prime Minister Micheal Manley that his party would not contest any election so long as the electoral system remained under the absolute control of the incumbent government.

The Prime Minister was overseas visiting the International Monetary Fund and the World Bank, and issued a statement that the electoral system of Jamaica was in need of some improvement, and on his return home, he will meet with the Leader of the Opposition on this. At the meeting on his return, the Prime Minister was accompanied by Ministers PJ Patterson and Keble Munn. Mr. Seaga's team included Mr. Bruce Golding and party stalwart and attorney-at-law, Mr. Abe Dabdoub.

The proposal by the Leader of the Opposition that the process should fall under the control of a national committee, with a membership team acceptable to both political parties, was adopted. It was also agreed that the other persons at that meeting would flesh out the details and advise the Prime Minister. There followed a period of discussion and exchange of letters.

Out of this consultation exercise the Electoral Advisory Committee was conceived, and its structure and authority determined and agreed. The EAC was created by an Act of the Parliament of Jamaica in August 1979. This Act removed the electoral system from under the absolute control of the government of the day.

This statute provides that the Governor General of Jamaica shall appoint all members to this body, and at meetings each member has one vote, and the chairman has a casting vote. The legislation also stipulated how individuals will qualify to be appointed to this committee. The Prime Minister and the Leader of the Opposition each had the right to nominate two persons. Three persons who are not active politicians were to be appointed by the Governor General after consultation with both political leaders; one of these shall be chairman.

The Director of Elections is to be appointed on the recommendation of the members of the committee, and be responsible for the operation of the Electoral Office which conducts and manages the electoral process, and would automatically become a non-voting member of the EAC, making a total of eight members.

This committee is charged by Parliament, to determine policy for the management of the Electoral Office and the electoral system and instruct the Director of Elections accordingly. The Director is obliged to carry out the policies of the EAC, and if he does not wish to do so he must advise Parliament. The EAC is also to provide the necessary staff, facilities, equipment and supplies to assist the Director to manage and conduct National Elections. The government is required to fund the operations of the committee.

This was a major step forward in protection of a democratic system to elect our political leaders, and remains so until today. It did not only remove the responsibility for the management and conduct of elections from the direct and total control of the government of the day, but also relieved it of the pressure of competitive partisan politics by placing it under the control of the EAC.

This committee was established over 45 years ago and from very early, a Parliamentary Precedent evolved and is now well entrenched. Reports are made by this committee to Parliament and any recommendations made are accepted and implemented. Any proposed changes would require the written agreement of the committee. This position taken by the elected representatives of the people has served to enrich the authority and has enhanced and imbued the decisions taken by the Electoral Advisory Committee with tremendous public confidence and trust.

This display of confidence by the Parliament of the country, in the decisions of that body, is a great credit to those who have been privileged to serve our country as members of this important committee. Special thanks are due to the early members. They established its operating standards and principles, and these have been observed by their successors.

Jamaicans appointed to the EAC from 1979 to 2005.

Prof. Hon. Gladstone E.M. Mills CD,OJ	Oct.9,79--May30,93	**Chairman # 2**
Mrs. Shirley Miller CD, OJ	Oct.9,79--May30,93	Selected Member **# 2**
Dr. Ronald V. Irvine MD,OBE, CD.	Oct.9,79--Dec.10,8	Selected. Member
Dr. Paul Robertson	Oct. 9,79--Oct1,91	Nominated Member
Mr. O. K. Melhado, CD	Oct. 9,79--Dec.10,80	Nominated Member
Mr. Bruce Golding	Oct.9,79 --Feb.8,84	Nominated Member
Mr. Abraham Dabdoub	Oct.9,79 --Nov.26,83	Nominated Member
	Dec10,97--May31,05	Nominated Member **# 3**
Mr. R. N. "Reg" Murray, CD	May15,80--Sept.3,85	Selected Member
Dr. D.K. Duncan	Jan.7,81 --Dec.8,81	Nominated Member
Miss. Portia Simpson	Dec.9,82 --Apr.25,90	Nominated Member **# 5**
Mr. Errol Anderson	May16,84 --Jan.21,87	Nominated Member
Mr. Karl Samuda CD	Feb.8,84 --Apr.25,90	Nominated Member
	June1,05 --**Present**	Nominated Member

Prof. Laurie H. E. Reid CD	May20,87--May12,93	Selected Member
Mr. Edmund Bartlett	July29,87--April 25,90	Nominated Member
Dr. Mavis Gilmour CD	Mar.19,87--July22,87	Nominated Member
Mr. Ryan G. Peralto CD	May 9,90--May31,05	Nominated Member **# 1**
Mr. Anthony Johnson	May 9,90--May1,96	Nominated Member
Mr. Donald Buchanan	May 9,90--May15,00	Nominated Member **# 4**
Dr. Peter Phillips PhD	Oct. 9,91--Nov1,95	Nominated Member
Mr. Peter J. Thwaites	Aug.11,93--Jan.5,94	**Chairman**
Mr. W.K "Don" Chin See. QC, CD	Aug.11,93	Selected Member
	May 10,94--July 27, 00	**Chairman**
Mrs. Pamela Benka - Coker QC	Aug.11,93--July 27, 96	Selected Member
Hon. Mrs. Corrine McLarty CD, OJ	May 2,94 --July 27, 00	Selected Member
Prof. Hon. Gerald C. Lalor CD, OJ	July 28,96--July 27,00	Selected Member
Mrs. Maxine Henry-Wilson	Jan. 25,93- - Nov.30,95	Nominated Member
Mr. Danville Davidson	May 1,96-- Dec.3,97	Nominated Member
Mr. Michael Peart	May 15,00 --Nov.15,02	Nominated Member
Prof. Hon. Errol L. Miller CD, OJ	Dec.18,00 --**Present**	**Chairman**
Dr. Herbert J. Thompson, PhD	Dec.18,00 --**Present**	Selected Member
Mrs. Dorothy Pine-McLarty	Dec.18,00 --**Present**	Selected Member
Mr. Linton Walters	Nov.15,02 --**Present**	Nominated Member
Mr. Burchell Whiteman	Dec. 1,03 --**Present**	Nominated Member
Mr. Thomas Tavares-Finson	June 1,05 --**Present**	Nominated Member

Directors of Elections --------- Secretaries to the E A C

Mr. C. W. Dundas	Dec.6,79 - Nov.12,80.	Mr. Roy Forbes	Nov.1,79-Oct.27,93.
Mr. Noel Lee, CD	Nov.19,80 - May12,93	Mrs. D. M. Black	May 4,94-Jul.21 .98.
Maj. W. Sutherland	Apr.4,94 -Sept.23,96	Miss Enid Clarke	Oct.6,98-July 31, 99.
Mr. A. Danville Walker	May26,97 -Present.	Miss Stacie Wong	Aug.1,99 — **Present.**

Chapter Eight

THE EAC AND THIS INVENTION

On May 1, 1990 I was appointed a member of the Electoral Advisory Committee of Jamaica by Governor General Sir Florizel Augustus Glasspole GCMG, GCVO, CD, ON, on the nomination of the Honourable Edward Philip George Seaga PC, O.N., the Leader of the Opposition.

When I introduced my thinking to a meeting that same month, the EAC decided to hold a **Retreat from June 30 to July 1, 1990** to review the performance of the electoral system. **This gave me the opportunity to make a comprehensive presentation of my proposed system to members and invitees at that retreat at the Stony Hill Hotel, and explain in detail how it would work.** A number of persons pointed out the need to take on board certain things that were part of the management process and we discussed how these could perhaps be best accommodated.

I wrote on July 23rd 1990 to Chairman Professor the Honourable Gladstone Mills, outlining my system concept and design, accommodating and incorporating the points made at the Retreat:-

Dear Professor Mills,

In keeping with my undertaking to provide to the Electoral Committee a proposal which would seek to identify the areas of voting procedure ,which may be computerized, to try to and remove or alleviate some of the problems which the nation has experienced with conducting elections, I am attaching a two page draft document, "Proposed Computerized Voting System for Jamaica."

As I proposed, a copy of this has been sent to Dr. Paul Robertson of the P.N.P., so that they may review it before our next meeting in order to determine if they wish to add or propose refinements when the proposal comes before the full committee.

As background, let me put on record some of my thinking and work including discussions held by me within my party on this subject of improvement to our electoral system, in an effort to protect the integrity of the system from fraudulent manipulation which has plagued what is basically a sound system designed to provide the framework for free and fair elections.

Since the week after the March 6, 1990 Parish Council Elections, I came to two fundamental conclusions.

First, the clear and blatant acts of fraud which plagued the elections of 1980, 1986, 1989 and 1990 could never be avoided by any system which relied so heavily on humans to guarantee its integrity.

Second, certain areas of the electoral laws and certain procedures and practices in the management of the electoral system will require new legislation and rules, if our democracy is to have a fair chance for survival, in the long run.

In answer to the first problem, I concluded that a system of computer voting, which ensured that the machine would replace human discretion to identify the citizen entitled to vote, record his/her vote alone, on only one occasion on any given election day, was basic to ensuring the principle of one man one vote. I was aware that computer ID by fingerprint was used to allow entrance to certain areas in a number of high security operations in the U.S.

It became clear that if it were possible to marry computer data storage, with fingerprinting ID, recording of votes, and storage and counting of votes, many current problems of our system would be addressed. You will recall that in May in discussions at the committee level, I had raised this idea.

The visit of the Electoral Committee Representatives to Venezuela in May has enabled Mr. Anthony Johnson, Mr. Donald Buchanan and yourself to have had a first-hand view of an electronic system which could satisfy this concept.

Mr. Johnson having been in comprehensive discussions with me on the idea was able to pursue detailed discussions which have satisfied him that our requirements can be met.

This process has led to the present unanimous agreement at our June retreat, to propose that a computerized system which can satisfy the concerns in the document, will give our nation an electoral system that can correct the peculiar problems which face us, especially in relation to voting procedure and the authenticity of the votes counted to determine the results of an election.

There is still the problem to ensure that the data base of information on persons reflects an accurate list of all persons 18 years and over, who are citizens normally resident in Jamaica who are entitled to vote.

The idea here is to provide a true and accurate list by collating the current electoral data with data of Births, Deaths and Immigration on a continuing basis and by deduction, be able to achieve the following:

a) *Produce a list of all persons resident in Jamaica over age 18 whose data is already in the system.*

b) *Produce a monthly list of persons, who have reached age 18 whose picture, and address would now be required to complete the data to place their finger-print on the voters' list.*

c) *This we have learnt is recognized and addressed by the proposal for a National Registration System.*

Finally, these proposals will provide a system that can keep us constantly aware of our voter population, and provide that population with a sense of privacy and security in pro-tection of their democratic voting rights.

Yours Sincerely,
Ryan G. Peralto

Attachments.

Draft.
PROPOSED COMPUTERISED VOTING SYSTEM FOR JAMAICA

1. *Module capable of storing ID information on all 1.2 million voters by name, address, finger mark, as well as candidates' name, picture, party symbol.*

2. *Module capable of accessing several different ballot choices, constituency, division, P.D.*

3. *Module capable of transmitting back to central control unit by AC/DC for a minimum of 12 hours each vote as it is registered by the module.*

4. *Module will generate a paper acknowledging voter's name, and the fact that the vote has been recorded after identifying the voter by finger mark and registering their vote.*

5. *Module to be operated by touch system identifying finger mark to register vote. Lever system available if required.*

6. *Module can provide at end of voting, a count of votes for each candidate and total ballots polled at that module with appropriate print out.*

7. *3000 interactive modules located across the island would allow voting by Electors, from any location for any constituency.*

8. *Unit operating at control centre will do the following:-*

   a) *Activate and terminate operation of all modules for the opening and closing of the poll. Receive confirmation of these actions.*

   b) *Be sensitized to identify if any module is rendered inoperative.*

   c) *Receive and store for final count individual votes, immediately persons vote at module.*

   d) *Provide a count, constituency by constituency, of the result of voting for the day, at the close of poll, with the appropriate print out.*

BENEFITS

1. *No duplicate voting possible, since each voter will only be able to register a vote if the voting module has identified his finger mark as a bona fide elector. Stuffing of ballot boxes will now be eliminated.*

2. *The programme of the system will ensure that after each elector in the system has voted, that finger mark will no longer be accessible to activate voting for the rest of the voting period.*

3. *Since all details of each voter are to be stored in the system, where ever the voter is in the island, the system will be able to recognize him, accept his vote, locate and count it, in the division or constituency which his records indicate. This will negate the effect of stealing ballot boxes since the person may vote at any station anywhere in the island.*

4. *The identification by finger mark will reduce the electoral personnel at each centre. One electoral official, to see that instructions are given to each voter for using the equipment, one*

representative of each political party, and one security officer to ensure that the equipment is in good working order and is not wantonly destroyed or otherwise rendered useless.

5. *Because of 10 by finger mark the time in voting procedure will be reduced by at least 50%.This will serve to reduce the number of polling stations from 6000 plus to around 3000. Far less personnel both electoral and security will be required to operate the system.*

6. *The demand on security forces at the module sites will be considerably reduced and therefore leave them free for patrolling to ensure that communities are not prevented access to a module to register their votes.*

7. *The counting of the election results at the end of the day will be almost instantaneous and will be available at the control centre.*

Signed: Ryan G. Peralto
July 16th 1990.

On 12 August 1990 the Electoral Advisory Committee at a meeting agreed that it was necessary because of the "technical sophistication" to appoint a sub-committee who with the assistance of technical persons, should examine my proposal to establish if the Technology and Equipment I identified existed, and if it was feasible and practical for them to be used to build such a system.

The sub-committee chaired by Professor Laurie Reid, with Dr. Peter Philips, the Director of Elections, Mr. Noel Lee and I as members, was charged to examine my proposal in detail, to determine if the technologies and equipment I had identified was available, and could be brought together to perform the functions that I had determined should be automated.

The sub-committee spent some twelve months, writing, speaking to, and visiting, potential suppliers, reputed experts, specialists, and some users of the component technologies, prior to making their report.

The sub-committee also sought the opinion and advice of local experts in computer and electronic data gathering and processing, namely Messrs. Sydney

Abrahams Jr., Patrick Terrelonge, and Douglas Halsall, on the feasibility of my proposals. This sub-committee made two written reports in 1991 as follows:

Professor Reid's Sub-Committee Report dated 22 August 1991

"In the interest of providing a fool proof electoral system, the Electoral Advisory Council has embarked on a search to provide a state-of-the-art ELECTORAL SYSTEM using the best tools available in the electoral data processing and security fields.

Advanced recognition devices will be used to ensure that pictorial and graphical data can be used to verify identification of the voter, both at the enumeration, and at time of actual voting in the polling station. At the polling station, once the recognition is verified and accepted, the central controlling data base will be queried for previous voting and if not, it will be updated so that only one vote per person will be available country wide.

The use of both foreign and local expertise as a prerequisite of the process will ensure that that technology transfer is effected, so that ongoing maintenance and enhancement of the system will be carried out.

The successful completion of this project will establish a saleable capability for this service for other countries (as we believe that only one other country is as advanced), and so significant royalty revenue could be earned through a joint venture between the successful vendors and the Government. To proceed with the process, the necessary policy approval and funding have to be in place, hence we submit our desired system overview and our draft pre-qualification advertisement which we hope to distribute through our High Commissions worldwide or by other suitable media. Your comments and suggestions are solicited".

The acceptance of this first report by the committee plus the agreement that the committee would proceed to request the financing that would be required to implement such a system led to a second report.

Professor Reid's Sub-Committee Report dated 29 August 1991

"In the interest of providing a fool proof and highly secure electoral system, the Electoral Council has embarked on a march to provide a state-of-the-art ELECTORAL SYSTEM using the best tools available in the electoral, data processing and security fields.

The past problems with breaches of security, where boxes and other items were taken from the proper hands, will be totally negated by the use of the proposed system. The authority to receive, update and transmit verification and permission to vote depends on a highly secure central data base system. Hence, remote security at the polling station will become very much less of a problem.

Advanced recognition devices will be used to ensure that pictorial and graphical data can be used to verify identification of the voter, both at enumeration and at time of actual voting in the polling station. Specifically, the voter's fingerprint will be captured and stored in a central database.

A subset of this global database will be duplicated for each polling station. The index finger will activate the module and once the recognition is verified and accepted, the central controlling data base will be queried for previous voting and if not, it will be updated so only one vote per person will be possible country wide. At the end of voting the local module will print and transmit the results for each candidate. Hence the final results, subject to security confirmation, will be available almost immediately after the polls have closed.

To prevent loss of data at the remote sites, an advanced power backup system will be installed, so that a full eight hours of power will be available.

There are already in use in Jamaica reliable means of communication. The inherent problems of transmission across our rugged terrain can be solved using this technology (called ground wave transmission, used extensively by armies). Also at least two other communication backup systems will be in 'place so that no data loss will ever occur. In any event, because the central data base will only be queried for previous voting status during the day and because the image storage will be at the on-site facility, the actual amount of data transmitted per second will be very manageable. This fact coupled with the average voting time of about 3 minutes per voter makes the central query facility feasible. (transmission query and approval time will be less than 30 seconds, the rest of the time is to allow for manual controls systems to be effected).

The use of both foreign and local expertise as a pre-requisite of the process will ensure that technology transfer is effected, so that on going maintenance and enhancement of the system will be carried out.

The successful completion of this project will establish a saleable capability for this service for other countries (as we believe only one other country is as advanced), and so some signif-icant royalty revenue could be earned through a joint venture between the successful vendors and the Government.

To proceed with the process the necessary policy approval, and funding will have to be in place, hence we respectfully submit this desired system overview and our draft Pre--Qualification advertisement which we hope to distribute through our High Commissions worldwide or be other suitable media".

Professor Reid's Sub-Committee also determined that the services of a technology company would be required to undertake the integration of the various technologies and different types of equipment in order to build this system.

The Reports of Professor Reid's Sub-Committee could not be faulted, despite attempts made in general discussions in meetings of the EAC to gently suggest that there may be a need to re-evaluate the proposal. This was never pushed too far as it would threaten the stability of the committee.

In addition a couple of members kept pursuing obvious delaying tactics, by sniping at aspects of the proposal, by attempts to trivialize the need for a automated system, and by questioning the wisdom of making what was anticipated would prove to be such a substantial capital investment in a pioneering effort.

Some members from meeting to meeting re-opened ground already covered. They also kept insisting that the attention of the committee should be concentrated on preparing for the holding of the next national elections.

It became clear that the majority of the members did not have the will to take the idea any further, despite the fact that there was no doubt that the concept could become a reality. One particular nominated member confidently expressed to me, that the system would not be accepted for use for a long time. My respect for a prophetic colleague has grown over time.

The term of the Selected Members of the EAC expired and new appointments were made. New officers were elected in the political parties and some nominated members were also changed.

The newest members took some time to get familiar with the operation and to read the records of the committee in order to bring themselves up to date. I once again took the opportunity to document on the 5th of April, 1993 my proposed system, this time in more specific terms as follows:-

THE PERALTO PROPOSAL FOR ELECTRONIC VOTING SYSTEM

(1) *Electronic identification of voters by reading their finger prints and matching these against their fingerprints on the data base.*

(2) *This enables that person, and that person alone, to access the Electronic System to do the following:*
  (a) Select the candidate of their choice(at this point a mistake can be corrected).
  (b) Vote for the candidate of their choice.

(c) *Get a receipt acknowledging that their vote has been recorded.*

(3) *Immediately the elector votes, the following also takes place in the computer memory.*
   (a) *The vote is recorded at the counting station for the candidate chosen and this trans-action in its entirety is also transmitted by code, directly to the main storage computer at another location, where it is also stored.*
   (b) *The voter's name is recorded and that voter's data base will be rendered inactive from that instant on, and inaccessible to anyone throughout the entire system.*

(4) *Since The System will be totally powered and Interlinked by Direct Line, Battery and Satellite it will also be possible to do the following:*
   (a) *A voter may vote at any station for any candidate.*
   (b) *When the System Identifies the voter, only the candidates in the constituency in which that voter registered are made available for choice.*
   (c) *The vote will then be automatically registered for the candidate chosen for the constituency in which the voter is listed.*
   d) *Where an elector votes outside their Polling Station and or the constituency in which they registered,his/her vote will not only be recorded by that voting station but will also be noted as belonging to the Polling Station and or constituency other than the Polling Station where the vote was cast.*

5) *The system will redirect the vote cast to the correct voting station.*

POLL BOOK/BALLOT COUNTING AT EACH POLLING STATION

The system will keep accumulating in its computer memory a record of the result of each access to the system on an accumulating basis. At the close of the Poll, the system will produce print-outs of the following at each Voting Station.
   (a) *A tally sheet showing the total votes cast for each Candidate by Elector listed at that Voting Station.*
   (b) *A list by names and address of all Electors listed at that station who voted at that station.*
   (c) *A list of all persons listed as Electors at that station but who voted at other stations, naming the station where those electors voted after including their vote in item (a).*
   (d) *A list by name and address of all other Electors in that constituency not listed at that station, who voted at that station naming the station to which their vote has been transferred.*

(e) *A list by name and address of all other Electors who also voted at that station for other constituencies and naming the constituency and station to which their vote has been transferred.*

(f) *Number of attempted accesses refused because that fingerprint was not in the Data Base".*

I was persuaded that an EAC Report to Parliament recommending the use of the system once submitted, would lead to early installation of this system. I was relying very heavily on the established tradition that whatever the EAC proposed to Parliament, to ensure that national elections are properly and fairly conducted, would be accepted and implemented without delay.

My conclusion, which later proved to be premature, was also based on various discussions at the level of the full committee from which, I was led to the view that a strong recommendation to move very quickly to implementation would be made in that report.

On 13 July, 1994 the Electoral Advisory Committee made a report to Parliament, and I now quote from pages 2 and 3 of that report as follows:-

"APPRAISAL.

At a Retreat in 1990, the Electoral Advisory Committee observed that the effectiveness of the present system was severely hampered by:

(a) The withdrawal of more qualified and civic minded citizens from involvement in the system, and

(b) The indisciplined, disruptive and fraudulent behaviour of certain groupings of citizens which had the effect of undermining the electoral process. As a result, the Committee has been exploring ways and means to develop reforms for implementaion.

In November 1991 (error August) a sub-committee under the Chairmanship of Professor L.H.E. Reid reported that a Computerized Voting System appeared to offer a real possibility of providing a competent and efficient system, secure against the abuses experienced over the years. This report was accepted by the Committee and extensive investigations into such a system began. The Committee has been considering the views of technical experts on the different elements involved as well as exploring the availability of such a system. The concept benefits and concerns regarding the proposed system are set out in detail on pages 19 to 22 where the election day process is examined.

In September 1993, the Committee formed the view that in addition to any change in the actual voting system, the administration of the electoral system needed to be restructured to ensure that it functioned effectively. A management audit was commissioned and after the Committee examined tenders, Price Waterhouse was selected to undertake the study with the following terms of reference:-

To examine and make recommendations in respect of:

--the system, procedures and resources required for the preparation of an accurate and reliable voters' list;

--Personnel requirements and compensation;

--the company best suited to carry out the Electoral Office's fingerprinting requirement.

--the computer hardware and software required to generate the necessary reports/lists on a timely basis to achieve the Electoral Office's objectives;

-- a suitable vendor to provide a national identification card.

The Committee further advised Price Waterhouse that the assessment of the suppliers of fingerprinting systems was of the highest priority, and that this needed to be concluded as quickly as possible.

Price Waterhouse submitted a series of interim reports in respect of each facet of the Terms of Reference, including an evaluation of senior staff, and, having had discussions with the Committee, a final report is soon to be presented."

After four years of explaining my concept again and again, arguing, cajoling, pleading and sometimes even quarrelling, my arguments and my concept were finally officially accepted and were formally supported by the EAC.

Perhaps the most important reference in the 1994 EAC report as far as the future of the proposed electoral system is concerned was this statement appearing on page 19.

"The Committee came to the view that a system which removed the important elements of the voting procedures from human intervention to an automated process offered the best prospect

to solve the problems and accepted the concept of a **Computerized Voting System."**

The necessary legislative action directed at giving effect to the 1994 EAC recommendations were taken by Parliament.

A technical sub-committee was again appointed on August 14, 1996 to examine the proposed new system, to see how best to proceed to get it in place.

Professor The Honourable Gerald Lalor, O.J. was appointed chairman. The other members were the four Nominated Members, and the Director of Elections. Mr. Michael Ho Sue of the U.W.I. was co-opted as a local expert to join the team and other persons were consulted during the investigations.

The next EAC Report to Parliament dated 24 April ,1996 concentrated on recounting the abuses of the system which coincided with my own assessment, and went on to recommend a host of very useful and important legal and management steps to be taken to deal with the persons who abuse the system.

When my colleague member Tony Johnson and I were invited and signed this report, we were disappointed that though it acknowledged that a system could be built to prevent the recognized abuses of the electoral process, it did not recommend any positive step to be taken immediately towards implementation of the proposed system. We, thereupon, felt compelled to submit a minority report stating our concerns. **I now quote the final three paragraphs of our submission:-**

"We, therefore, view the Legal Reforms which are proposed as an attempt to address Election Day problems, as inadequate to provide realistic and effective measures to ensure our citizens right to select their representatives in FREE AND FAIR ELECTIONS".

The opportunities to corrupt the system remain. Those who corrupt it may be caught and may be suitably punished. That is not enough. WE NEED A SYSTEM TO SUBSTANTIALLY PREVENT OR AVOID THE CORRUPTION. We, therefore, at this time do not support the proposed reforms to address

election day offences. We see this as only accommodating and facilitating the possible use of the present Election Day process which remains condemned by the EAC and the nation at large, as being manifestly corrupt".

Little did Tony and I realize at the time that the very real and protracted struggle to get the system in place and used in elections, was just starting, and would go on for over fifteen years.

Perhaps deep down we may have sensed that the process would be deliberately drawn out, but we were hoping that in the national interest and out of respect for the principle of fair play, good sense would soon prevail.

Some recommendations of this report included the establishment of a judicial committee to expedite treating with offences from nomination day to election day, the establishment of a Registration Centre in each constituency to facilitate Continuous Registration of electors to be able to maintain an up-to-date Voters List to be published twice per year, plus new fines and new penalties to punish abusers of the process during the election period, including postponement and/or the voiding of elections in any or all constituencies or part thereof. **The early creation of a Electoral Commission to replace the EAC was also recommended**.

Legislation was promptly put in place establishing the process of **Continuous Registration**, the new offences and **more severe penalties attached to abuse of the voting process**, to establish the quasi-judicial tribunal, the "**Constituted Authority**" and to provide for the appointment of three judges to form a Election Court to take early decisions on election complaints. A **process to speedily address Voting Day offences was finally in place**. These were all available and used for the first time for the 1997 Election.

At about two o'clock on the morning of the December 18, 1997 Parliamentary Elections, I was at the JLP party office when we received lists of electors who were to be included on what was supposed to be the official Voters List to be used that day. We had to sort these into batches by parish and dispatch drivers to take them to our candidates in the different constituencies.

While the sorting was being done, some official ballot papers, to be used to vote for candidates that day, were found in the cartons in which the lists of additional electors were received.

I immediately advised the Electoral Office of the discovery of official ballot papers, in the cartons which they had sent to us, and requested that they come and take possession of them, and notified the party leader. The sorting of those lists was completed, after the Electoral Office removed all ballot papers, and they were then sent by cars to the different constituencies in the parishes.

I believe even now that an attempt was made to set up the party as seeking to steal that election. I believe the intention was to report to the Police that unmarked ballot papers were missing. Then an official search of our party premises since documents were sent to us, would unearth the missing ballots. The media would take immense pleasure to run with that news for weeks and this would totally discredit our party and unhinge our efforts to get reform of the actual voting system, a struggle which I had personally taken on and which I was also pursuing as a representative of the political party of which I was a member.

The next EAC Report to Parliament dated October 12, 1999, recommended more legislative amendments affecting **Voter Registration and Membership of the "Constituted Authority"**, specified the **time between nomination day and voting day, and introduced sanctions against Presiding Officers** and the authority to **Void the Poll**. It also reported on the progress being made in implementing Phase1, the new ERS that was the subject of a contract dated 8 June 1996, and was now expected to be completed by March 2000.

I pause here to state that I was well aware, at the outset and again at the present time, that some highly placed individuals in both of the political parties are not in favour of implementing this system.

I had always anticipated that attempts would be made to frustrate efforts at having the new system implemented. Persons integral to the electoral process do not support the use of an automated system to prevent the abuses. Some such persons were then and some are again in a position to frustrate its implementation. I did not anticipate the extent to which they will go to delay this effort. They did so then, in quite not-so-subtle but very effective ways, and these will do so again.

Oh what a tangled web some of us are capable of weaving, as we smile and are so courteous and even verbally supportive of the proposed new system, while taking action or failing to take action, in order to delay and hopefully to frustrate efforts directed at advancing its implementation.

After Professor Reid's Committee Report of August 1991 until July 1993, the EAC took no positive action towards implementing this system or any part of it, despite accepting that it could be built and would be capable of ensuring "one man one vote" and only registered electors would be allowed to vote. The will and the courage to proceed towards building the system proved impossible to summon in the majority of the sitting EAC members.

This was perhaps partially due to unfamiliarity, and a lack in information and understanding, on the part of the majority of the members at that time of the massive technological advances that had been made, in electronic storage and processing of information, transmission of data, as well as automated recognition devises.

It is fair to say that after submitting the 1994 Report to Parliament, which was made within three months of the new members of the committee taking office, the EAC for the most part became entwined in analyzing the audit report on the electoral office and all things that flowed from it. Some very good practical changes were agreed on as a result. This was a useful exercise.

Changes in the management processes are not, cannot, and will never be substitutes for reforms needed to plug the loop holes in the voting process, but they have made the existing system more efficient and effective.

In my view, the reforms implemented between 1996 and 2004 particularly since 1999 under the new Director of Elections, have contributed substantially to the establishment and development of perhaps the most efficient electoral management unit in the democratic world, despite not installing the new voting process.

The decision to concentrate the energies of the EAC on improving the processes and procedures needed, to properly conduct elections, was greatly influenced by all kinds of investigations, analyses, and reports. This documentation was prepared originally to accurately tie down minute details of the specifications of the new system to ensure efficient and effective implementation and operation. It resulted in reforms and refinements to various processing procedures used by the electoral office, to prepare for, and conduct elections, and were based on technical official studies, and those recommendations have all been taken on board.

In 1995, some firms responded to specifications sent by the EAC detailing the system we wished to build. Some of these companies at the invitation of the Committee visited with us, in November that year, to demonstrate what they were in a position to offer, which was mainly incomplete prototypes of their interpretation of the specifications provided.

Five companies visited and demonstrated what they had put together as a possible system, namely **Thomas De La Rue,** a U.K. company, and four US companies, **Polaroid Inc., Business Technology Systems Ltd and Management Support Technology Inc., and IDMATICS Inc.**

The members of the EAC, the management team of the EOJ, the movers and shakers in the nation, political leadership, civil society, the media, all were able to see, most for the very first time in their lives, the technologies and equipment operating carrying out their specialist functions efficiently. It was also clear that we had some distance to go towards building the system designed.

The EAC commissioned from Price Waterhouse in Jamaica a technical report on the demonstrations. After considering this report, the EAC decided it would be best to approach implementation of the Electronic Voting System by contracting a company to work to the specifications of the EAC. This company would acquire and marry the different elements contained in the design to produce a synchronized and fully integrated system. However, the building of the system would be approached on a phased basis and the specification for each phase was agreed.

Phase 1

This is essentially the creation of a database comprising all registered electors in which all the data, inclusive of fingerprints, would be electronically cross matched to remove duplicates, and then to electronically store the complete set of this information on the system. This would ensure that a voters list produced from that database would have each person listed once only and at that person's correct address. **This phase has come to be referred to as the "ERS" (Elector Registration System).**

Phase 2

This would be to expand and configure the system, to provide it with the ability on voting day to capture and cross match the elector's fingerprint and other data, in order to identify each elector before it would issue an official ballot paper on which the elector marks an X beside the name of the chosen candidate. **This phase has come to be referred to as the "EVIBIS". (Electronic Voter Identification and Ballot Issuing System).**

Phase 3

This would be to configure that database so that on voting day after electors have been identified by their live fingerprints by the equipment they will then be permitted by it, to select one of the candidates displayed on a computer screen using their live fingerprints. Then the equipment will credit that vote to the candidate chosen, and issue to each elector a slip, with the name of the candidate credited with that vote. The slip of paper issued is to ensure that the elector sees who is credited with his/her vote. That slip will carry an official identification mark, but it will not have anything on it that can be used to identify the elector who casts that vote. The voter is then required to fold the slip of paper and drop it into a ballot box. After the close of the poll, the slips will serve as an audit trail to be compared with the results of the votes for each candidate as published and printed by the equipment. This phase has come to be referred to as "Electronic Voting".

After this was agreed, the EAC proceeded to try to find a company prepared to contract to follow specifications provided by the EAC and build the system beginning with Phase 1, as well as to establish the cost for so doing.

The EAC also decided at that time, that a major effort should be immediately directed at legal reforms, to deal with persons who abuse the electoral system, and to work at having a good and accurate Voters List in time for the holding of Parliamentary Elections expected in 1997/98.

A substantial review of all legislation governing the conduct of elections was undertaken to put in place procedures, to handle the expected breaches in the upcoming election, and to address operational and legal reforms which would be required to enable Phase 1 to be used to produce a clean Voters' List.

The 1996 decision to contract a company to implement Phase 1 ensured the production of an accurate Voters' List in the immediate future. I still believe that the development of Phases 1 & 2 should have been undertaken at one and the same time. The inherent weaknesses of the actual voting process, was relegated to taking place sometime in the future. The committee would not take on the challenge of addressing in a practical systemic way the prevention of the voting procedure irregularities.

Then a problem arose in selecting the company to undertake integrating the elements and build the system. As previously mentioned, some companies during the years the proposal was being evaluated, had examined my proposal and displayed, a degree of familiarity with the technologies and equipment identified to build the system, as well with the demands of the voting procedure.

TRW, of the Systems Integration Group from the USA also visited Jamaica but did not demonstrate the use of any equipment and had no exposure to the demands of any electoral system. However, they were chosen to build the system.

I was convinced that in making that decision the members of the Electoral Advisory Committee had not displayed the objectivity of a purist, which is required in deciding on such critically important matters.

Tony and I made it abundantly clear that the decision was not supported by us. As a member of the team examining exactly what that company had to offer, and while pursuing negotiations, to lead to the signing of a contract to build Phase 1, I was convinced after a few meetings that the wrong company was chosen and again made the EAC members aware of this.

I believe even now that to reject all those companies who had visited and demonstrated prototypes, which should normally have given them an edge to be considered to undertake the con-

tract, was imprudent. I believe the fact that I had spoken with some of those on my own and before other members even knew they existed, some before I became an EAC member. This together with the arguments in favour of choosing from those put forward by my colleague Mr. Anthony Johnson and I, spawned a fear of possible selective tailoring of the capabilities of the technologies, and created political suspicion and that eliminated them from serious and objective consideration.

That decision caused me to immediately develop major concerns about the implementation of the system should it be left to the guidance of that team. Between March 1996 and December 1997, the contribution of Danville Davidson a comptuer specialist, who was my colleague on the EAC proved to be invaluable when the teachings of the invention was being tailored to satisfy the operational requirements of the EOJ. These included settling on the processes, programmes, and equipment to be used, to build and install a composite system as Phase 1 of the Jamaican electoral system,.

The Reports to Parliament dated 24 April 1996, and 12 October 1999, included some important changes to be made, to operational procedures for better management of the process, and were very substantially directed at addressing Legal Reforms aimed at imposing punitive measures, and increasing penalties against persons who abuse the system, as well as to expedite dealing with voting day infringements and abuses.

The Jamaican Parliament passed legislation in 1999 to change the nominations to this committee that can be made by both the Prime Minister and the Leader of the Opposition, to one substantive member and one alternate who only has voting rights if their substantive colleague is absent. The selected members representing civil society, now effectively have control over the decision making process of the Electoral Advisory Committee. Implementing these changes over the next few years improved the legislation, the structure, and the processes used to operate our electoral system.

In the new millennium, membership of the EAC was again due to be appointed. Selected Members appointed in 2002 were, Chairman Professor Errol Miller C.D, Dr. Herbert Thompson and Mrs. Dorothy Pine McLarty. Two new alternate Nominated Members, Mr. Michael Peart and Mr. Abe

Dabdoub who had served as a founding member of the committee, were appointed to join Mrs. Maxine Henry-Wilson and I. Mr. A. Danville Walker was appointed Director of Elections.

In my opinion, the Jamaican System as at the end of 2004 was far better than most. This is a credit to the efforts of the Director of Elections. He had in place a fine cadre of management personnel who had established a set of systems and procedures, under the oversight and guidance of a very committed EAC team especially since 2002. These processes were functioning efficiently and effectively at all operational levels — — the Committee, the Secretariat, the EOJ and substantially so in the Field. This should not be taken to mean the absence of problems or differences and competing views that arise from time to time, but the national interest takes pride of place in arriving at solutions.

This committee had moved for the expeditious completion of Phase 1 and the refinements to its capability, while at the same time ensuring implementation of the reforms to the management procedures, processes, and legislative changes and additions agreed on over the years.

The EAC commissioned the building of a prototype of **Phase 2**, the **EVIBIS and on 19 June, 2003 it was officially used for the first time anywhere in the world, in the Saint Andrew Eastern constituency for the Parish Council Elections. It performed at an evaluated level of 98% success**. The shortfall resulted from it not being used for a period in one location, as the equipment was not made operational in time for the start of the voting. The manual process had to be used until the new system was activated.

The EAC agreed that the EVIBIS be used in the next Parish Council Election which is the next National Election due December 2006, and in all elections from then on.

The next time that the EVIBIS saw action was in the by-election which took place in Kingston Western on April 13, 2005. Here now is the report to the Electoral Advisory committee by the technical team of the Electoral Office of Jamaica:-

KINGSTON WESTERN BY-ELECTION - APRIL 13, 2005

INTRODUCTION

The overall performance of the **EVIBIS** *System in the Kingston Western By-Election exceeded expectation. A total of 113 workstations (computers) were used to cover the 152 polling stations. At the opening of polls thirty-four (30%) of the one hundred and thirteen (70%) workstations were not operational at 7:00 am.*

SETUP

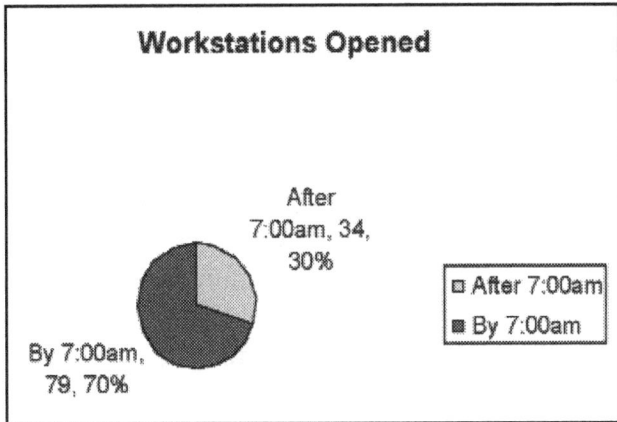

Workstations Opened

After 7:00am, 34, 30%

☐ After 7:00am
■ By 7:00am

By 7:00am, 79, 70%

Twenty-two of the workstations which opened late were located in high risk areas and as such were deployed late. There were also other problems that escalated the open time for some of the workstations within this group, such as electricity outage (breaker tripping) at Chetolah Park Primary where workstations for PS # 45 & 46 were affected. Two of the rooms were not opened at Denham Town Basic School (PS # 21-24) and a finger print scanner was replaced at Denham Town Clinic (PS # 17-20). Both St. Anne's Primary School (PS # 25, 26 & 28-30) and All Saints Infant (PS # 91-97) had late starts due to human error, on the part of the technicians, who panicked due to the boisterous nature and size of the crowd in trying to configure the machines.

There were also six printer-related problems which were quickly resolved by the technicians.

DURING THE DAY

During the course of the day, problems were experienced with three printers and three scanners that were either replaced or re-configured to resolve the problem. At three locations we had intermittent power outages due to the load on the circuitry with the New Testament Church Hall being the most problematic

The detailed report on each voting station showed that there were 17,565 electors on the Voters List and 9, 772 voted, which is 55.63%. Of those who voted 97.3% were processed by the EVIBIS; the other 2.7% were processed manually, when some machines were not operating, due to power supply problems experienced during the course of the day.

Without any further questioning, the performance of the EVIBIS on the occasion of these two official elections satisfied those who wish to put an end to vote stealing but may have had reservations about being able to build a system that could successfully carry out the processes.

The EAC then directed the EOJ to carry out the modifications to the database of electors necessary to facilitate the use of the EVIBIS in all voting stations and also started the acquisition of some of the additional computers, printers, fingerprint scanners, and dongles, that will be needed to facilitate its use in the Parish Council Elections due in 2006.

The money required to recruit and train personnel to operate the voting stations and to purchase additional equipment to enable the EOJ to use the EVIBIS islandwide amounts to some US$ 10 million. It is to be noted, that once the EVIBIS is to be used islandwide, the number of Voting Stations is to be reduced by nearly 45% and voting day personnel by some 30%, effecting substantial savings that would be recurrent. The time needed to recruit and train personnel to manage Phase 2 Voting Stations should take no more than three months.

I proposed a timetable in 2004 to have the personnel required to operate Voting Stations islandwide selected, trained and ready to function at the latest December 2005. Acquiring and programming the equipment should take 12 weeks approximately.

The EVIBIS will substantially improve the system. However, the problems plaguing the Jamaican system for over half a century can best be permanently corrected by using Phase 3, "Electronic Voting Jamaica Style" to conduct voting.

To date, approximately US $ 23 million has been invested in the total system. Having Implemented the ERS, with the EVIBIS to come now, leaves only fingerprint voting just a software and a machine away. The job that is the duty of the EVIBIS is being performed by a machine now. This is being used by the US Immigration Department in Fort Lauderdale. This is what our Phase 2 will be like.

When Phase 3 is implemented, it will restore the absolute trust and confidence of our people in the integrity of the results of our elections in every Polling Station and in every Constituency, and will promote trust and confidence in each new administration regardless of political affliliation.

Chapter Nine

THE RIGHTS TO THIS INVENTION U.S. PATENT 5,878,399
PATENT APPLICATION FILED ON AUGUST 12, 1996 —
GRANTED ON MARCH 2, 1999

This is as good a point as any in this story, to speak definitively to the ownership of the Intellectual Property Rights contained in this system.

First, let me say that the Patent, which I was granted three years after application, covers more than the voting system described in the example detailed in the application itself, which explains how the teachings of this invention can be used to prevent abuses of the Jamaican electoral process.

On pages 5 and 6 of the grant of Patent, it clearly states the extent and scope of the protection granted to the Patent holder as follows:-

"While the invention has been described with particular reference to the preferred embodiment, it will be understood by those skilled in the art that various changes may be made and equivalents may be substituted for elements of the preferred embodiment without departing from the invention. For example, while finger print identification is believed to be very highly reliable, the system is adaptable to hand prints, thermal patterns, DNA, and other forms of identification as well. In addition, many modifications may be made to adapt a particular situation and material to a teaching of the invention without departing from the essential teachings of the present invention."

As is evident from the foregoing description, certain aspects of the invention are not limited to the particular details of the examples illustrated, and it is, therefore, contemplated that other modifications and applications will occur to those skilled in the art. For example, the computerized voting system is adaptable to other uses, such as a security system for military installation, schools, hospitals or the like, or as an inventory control system for aircraft parts, or controlled substances and

parts, for example. It is accordingly intended that the claims shall cover all such modifications and applications and do not depart from the true spirit and scope of the invention".

As someone who had in the late 1960s designed and developed a few construction systems, but was only made aware much later that I could have established patent rights to those and be compensated for their use by others in addition to benefiting from my own use of them, I was anxious from the moment I completed this system design that legal rights to this invention be established.

I was motivated to design this system, primarily to prevent abuses of the electoral system. I quickly recognized that being an executive of the Jamaica Labour Party, if I established legal rights before offering it for use to correct the problems of Jamaica's electoral system, that the chances of it being accepted, much less used, was as good as a snowball surviving in hell. I was sanguine in the belief that to first establish ownership, and then to offer that Jamaica could use it "free of charge", would cause the members of the other political party, (as a direct result of the politics of the 1970s), to feel a self imposed obligation to oppose its use.

I, therefore, waited until I offered my invention to the Electoral Advisory Committee and they were satisfied it could be used to provide a better System to conduct Elections, and then pointed out the real need to patent the system.

My children and I agreed very early that since it was my involvement in politics that led me to invent the system to identify individuals, and establish controls, to ensure that certain activities were carried out personally only by them that any earnings from its use for electoral purposes outside of Jamaica, would be used to provide, more and better education for Jamaicans, help to preserve our democracy, and no financial earnings would come to us.

In meetings of the Electoral Advisory Committee and its sub-committees, I raised on many occasions the need for these legal rights to be formally established. The Professor Reid Sub-Committee Report of August 22, 1991 addresses this. However, the EAC consistently failed to take any action in this regard.

After 1991 it is a fact that little or no progress was made to do anything about implementing the system. It was not until the members and the chairmanship of the committee changed in 1994 that serious and objective discussions resumed under the chairmanship of Mr. W.K. "Don" Chin See.

During the very first discussion in 1996 with the representatives of the company selected to build Phase 1, the negotiating team of the EAC was advised by that company, that they intended to contract the services of other firms who had specific expertise in the various technologies and equipment, and they would see to the integration of these to build a seamless operating system.

I immediately again raised the question of patenting the invention before someone else did so, especially as we would now be exposing the details of its design to others. The company told us that they would have their legal advisors, one of whom was present at the meeting, examine this before they could discuss that matter any further.

At a subsequent meeting held shortly after, their lawyer in response to the proposal put forward by Chairman Chin See that the system be patented jointly by the EAC and that company, told us that there was nothing to patent, as I did not physically have a system. I pointed out the international decision taken years earlier to recognize and grant protection to Intellectual Property.

The company insisted that there was nothing to be patented in what I had developed. Some of my colleagues appeared happily relieved and accepted that position. I was far from being amused unlike some members of our negotiating team. However, I suppose it was politically convenient for them once they heard the position taken by the company lawyer to accept that opinion.

I now replicate a letter written by me to Chairman Chin See on 20 September 1995, the year before those negotiations began.

Dear Mr Chin See,

Re: Patenting the Electronic Electoral System.

I am very concerned that as we continue to pursue with suppliers the possible implementation of the Electronic Electoral System, conceptualized and basically designed by me, that we run the risk of having the system patented by some overseas or local entity and marketed for electoral or commercial use.

In keeping with our earlier discussions I am therefore proposing that the Electoral Advisory Committee immediately take steps to have the system patented along the following lines: -

(a) The patent be registered in the name of the Electoral Advisory Committee and its successors.

(b) That a Trust be established by the Electoral Advisory Committee from the royalties received from other users of the system.

(c) That no royalty be collected arising from the use of the system as part of the electoral system for Jamaica.

(d) That this Trust be managed and administered by the members of the Electoral Advisory Committee, selected and appointed, and by a representative appointed by me and after my death by surviving members of my family in perpetuity. I am also proposing that the responsibilities of the Trust be: -

(i) To develop, manage and maintain an Educational Programme on the vital importance of maintaining at all times an electoral system which ensures Free and Fair Elections recognizing that this is the fundamental and basic element to the maintenance of a democratic system of government.

(ii) To offer scholarships to High School Students tenable at U.W.I., C.A.S.T. or any similar local Tertiary Educational Institution to pursue degree courses in:-
    (a) Public Administration
    (b) Research and Development aimed at developing and exploiting Jamaica's Natural Resources
    (c) Political Science
(iii) Educational Institutions for Technical Training.

THAT ALL INDIVIDUAL BENEFICIARIES OF THE TRUST WORK FOR AT LEAST TWO YEARS IMMEDIATELY FOLLOW-ING GRADUATION WITH A GOVERNMENT RECOGNIZED LOCAL TERTIARY EDUCATIONAL INSTITUTION OR WITH THE GOVERNMENT OF JAMAICA.

I am sure, Mr. Chairman, that the Electoral Advisory Committee appreciates the importance of patenting the system especially against the background of the increasing utilization of technology in the world.

As more and more countries adopt democracy worldwide, they will find that the use of an efficient and safe system to ensure one man one vote, same man same vote, is a vital necessity to the maintenance of a democratic system of Government. This system if patented and owned by Jamaica will position our country to reap substantial financial benefit from its use.

You will appreciate that as the person who conceptualized and designed the system that I am most anxious to have the system patented. I must advise therefore that unless the Electoral Advisory Committee moves within the next four weeks to have the system patented I will have been left with no choice but to have the system patented by me. However, I wish to make it clear that should I find it necessary to patent the system myself, I will also proceed to set up a Trust with the responsibilities outlined above.

Yours faithfully,
Senator Ryan. G. Peralto

I now quote from the minutes of the EAC Meeting of 11 October 1995:-

"III Patenting the Electronic System"

The Committee discussed a letter from Senator Peralto seeking to have the electronic system patented. The general consensus was that the Committee should not get involved in a matter of this nature and that Senator Peralto was free to do as he saw fit. His presence on the Committee is not considered prejudicial.

He was asked to leave the meeting during the discussions and is to be formally advised of the Committee's decision.

On 22 November, 1995, EAC Chairman Mr. Don Chin See replied thus:-

Dear Senator Peralto,

Patenting of Electronic Election System

Your letter 20th September 1995, to the Electoral Advisory Committee in regard to the above matter was considered. We understood, appreciated and agreed on the points made but considered that the EAC ought not to engage in this kind of activity.

On the other hand we recognize that Intellectual Property Rights are deserving of protection in the national interest and therefore advise that we have no objection to your patenting the system.

Yours Sincerely,
William K. Chin See

I wrote the E.A.C on 19 June 1996, in respect of the contract being negotiated with the selected integrator as follows:

PROPOSED DRAFT CONTRACT

I have a serious concern about the proposed Contract to be entered into with TRW to provide a new enumeration system particularly in relation to Article 30.

The Electoral Advisory Committee is seeking a Contractor to integrate certain technologies to provide a system which has been designed by identifying and using established technologies to reform the enumeration process in order to address the problems which have plagued this process to date.

The Contract is to integrate the various technologies and to develop the methodologies by which they can be configured to meet out requirements, and to provide that system.

Apart from the use of existing Hardware and Software, the supplier will develop specific Software and fine-tune the EAC's work process and programme, to accommodate efficient integration of the technologies to carry out particular functions to achieve in this case a particular result, which is a clean voters' list.

It is my view that all the things developed or produced under this Contract, for which the EAC is paying the supplier in order to meet the specifications of the EAC, should be owned by Jamaica.

If an employee is carrying out the instructions of a Company develops a product or process, the Company has ownership rights. The use of software developed for the system should not therefore:

(1) be subject to any restriction whatsoever on the Government for any particular use to which they may be put.

(2) nor attract additional cost depending on the volume of such use.

Any other items necessary to integrate the system and to operate it, which are already developed and owned by third parties and which attract a charge for supply or a user fee are a legitimate expense.

In summary, ownership of Software Programmes and Procedures developed to our specification to satisfy our design and needs, should reside in Jamaica, and then benefits of marketing accruing there from should accrue to Jamaica.

Yours Sincerely
Senator Ryan. G. Peralto.

On 26 June 1996, I was again obliged to write Chairman Chin See as follows:-

"INTELLECTUAL PROPERTY RIGHTS TO THE PROPOSED COMPUTERISED VOTER REGISTRATION SYSTEM

Dear Mr. Chin See,

Attached to the EAC minutes of June 19th.1996 is an appendix "Rights to the system concept and soft ware Programmes". It is to be carefully noted that that after all the negative arguments put forward by T.R.W on this matter, the proposed supplier in item 5 on page 1 ,makes the following proposal in order to establish legal rights to the system.

"The contractor proposes that Copyright and other Intellectual Property in the system design documentation and in the Software Programmes developed for the system vest in it. (meaning the contractor, and in return for this right to ownership the contractor proposes) and that the customer takes etc, etc."

It must now be abundantly clear, that that there is in fact Intellectual Property to be protected and exploited for financial gain.

As I advised some weeks ago, I have initiated steps to protect the Intellectual Property Rights to the system for Jamaica, by proceeding to register ownership of the system at my expense. I shall be setting up a Trust along the lines of my letter on this matter dated

20/9/95 and in keeping with the EAC's considered position, expressed in your letter dated 21/11/95, not to seek to establish Intellectual Property Rights and to agree that I may proceed to do so on my own.

It is also clear that there will be a great marketing advantage, to anyone who obtains the right to produce this system for third parties, to be able to use the Jamaica installation, which will be the first of its kind in the world, for exposing and demonstrating the actual system to potential buyers.

T.R.W is proposing contract terms and a commission side agreement which would enable them to control the rights to the system and in turn to give approval to the Jamaica Government to use it. They further propose that if and when the Jamaican facility is used to demonstrate the system to potential buyers, that in such circumstances and only in such circumstances, they would be prepared to pay a 2% commission on any sales resulting from this, to the Jamaican Government. They have further excluded sales to the Australian and South African markets from being able to attract any commission payable to the Jamaican Government. This immediately further restricts the potential of Jamaica benefiting from the use of this system, if acquired by third parties. Such is the nature of the commission agreement which they seek to sign. South Africa has a clear and urgent need for such a system.

T.R.W. is to be contracted to integrate certain technologies, specific processes, and design concepts, proposed and detailed by me and accepted by the EAC, to create a particular system for the EAC, which has been detailed by the EAC, in its RFP and Operational Plan.

T.R.W will, in the process of accomplishing this objective in order to supply the system, employ the use of hardware and software developed and owned by others, for which payment arrangements have been proposed in the contract.

T.R.W will also have to engineer and develop Software, and may refine procedures of the EAC, in order to produce a totally integrated and fully efficient operational system to meet the demands of the EAC, in accordance with the EAC's requirements and objectives. The system when produced must be compatible to be integrated into a Electronic Voting System, if agreed. Charges are included in the proposed contract value for this work. Any development and procedures resulting there from should therefore belong to the EAC, as these will, the product of work done as apart of a contract for hire.

I have already made it clear that that the EAC can make arrangements to use all of my developments to contract for the production of the system for the purpose of reforming the Electoral System without any obligation for the payment of royalty or licence. That commitment is firm and irrevocable.

Any agreement entered into with T.R.W, should not therefore provide to T.R.W any ownership rights in the system produced to meet the design and specifications proposed and agreed on by the EAC, as outlined in the RFP sent by the EAC to all potential suppliers. This has been now more carefully explained and agreed with T.R.W.

A commission contract to use the Jamaican installation for demonstration purposes which provides a benefit to Jamaica is in order; as is a contract to produce and install the system for the Government of Jamaica.

Yours truly,
Senator Ryan. G. Peralto

This firm was contracted as an integrator to follow the teachings of the invention and build a Elector Registration System for Jamaica. They engaged the services and arranged for use of technologies and expertise provided by others, to implement Phase 1 and had ensured that those involved in building this phase understood that it had to be compatible to be extended into Phases 2 and 3. In fact, special licence agreements had to be entered into with Cogent Systems Inc. of California, USA with respect to their fingerprint processing, storage, and cross matching technologies and the relevant operating programmes. Similarly, arrangements had to be made with Novoteric Inc. of Canada, and other suppliers, in respect of their operating programmes, to provide the kind of storage and manipulation of the database that is needed to facilitate the electoral process, so that these can be used on a continuing basis by the Electoral Office of Jamaica.

I now quote from Cogent Systems Inc. "Statement of Work" dated 6 January 2003, submitted by them when they were being contracted to work for, and to the specifications of, the Electoral Office of Jamaica, to produce the prototype of Phase 2, the Elector Voter Identification and Ballot Issuing System to be used in a pilot. (EVIBIS)

"The Jamaica Electoral Automation Program has been an ongoing effort since 1996. The total project is planned in three evolutionary and progressive phases, with each phase providing additional capabilities. Under the Phase1 implementation the elector's identity is verified through automated fingerprint matching technology during the registration process and Voter Identification cards are issued.

The Phase 1 implementation was carried out by TRW Inc. in 1997. Cogent Systems was a supplier to TRW under the Phase 1 effort, in that Cogent's fingerprint encoding and matching algorithms were modified by TRW and implemented in the Phase1 Electoral Registration System **(ERS).**

In Phase 2, the registered electors will be identified at the polls using the Automated Electronic Voter Identification and Ballot Issuing System **(EVIBIS)** *which will issue authenticated ballots for voting.*

During Phase 3 the electors identity will be verified at the voting booth itself and the elector will be permitted to vote electronically.

A number of milestones have been achieved under the Jamaica Electoral Automation Program. The Phase I system is fully operational and the program emphasis has now begun a transition to the Phase 2 implementation. The Phase 1 **ERS** *Central Site system is configured in Kingston, and 67 Enrollment Fix Centers are configured throughout the country. The* **ERS** *system has processed approximately 1.3 million citizens and Voter Identification cards have been distributed. Although Phase 2 is next to be implemented a need also exists to maintain the* **ERS** *Phase 1 operational capability to ensure continued elector registration success. A recent database conversion effort has identified multiple discrepancies within the* **ERS** *database calling into question the system reliability of the fingerprint matching solution employed under the Phase I* **ERS.**

Implementation of the Phase 2 **EVIBIS** *will be comprised of two components. (1) a Proof of Concept Pilot Programme, and (2), the Deployment and Operations program. The* **EVIBIS** *Pilot Program will consist of the production and delivery of 60* **EVIBIS** *units for evaluation of use during a Local Government Election. After validating the Pilot program's success the system will be deployed nationwide under the Deployment and Operations program.*

This Statement of Work (SOW) identifies the services and deliverables Cogent Systems Inc. will provide to the Electoral Advisory Committee (EAC) in support of the Phase 2 Pilot Program Implementation. Specifically this SOW addresses the production and delivery of 60 **EVIBIS** *units for the Phase 2 Pilot Program. Implementation and support for the Deployment and operations program is to be addressed under a separate Statement of Work based upon the EAC authorization to proceed with the subsequent phase of the programme."*

The Education and Electoral Foundation of Jamaica Limited was formed by me along with the other sitting members of the EAC in 2004.

The EEFJL is licensed to collect all royalties generated from the use of the invention for electoral purposes. It will use those

resources to assist in the advancement of the Education of Jamaicans, and to help the EAC to ensure that our people can participate in elections that are conducted in a manner that is "Free and Fair and Free from Fear", and also to foster the maintenance and support for democratic governance and the democratic system of government in Jamaica.

A licence was granted by The Education and Electoral Foundation of Jamaica Limited to The Electoral Advisory Committee (**EAC**) to permit use of the system to conduct Jamaican elections. The licence provides that the EAC may use the system to conduct elections in Jamaica at a cost of one Jamaican dollar as royalty stipulated in the licence I granted to the EEFJL.

This step was taken to satisfy and formalize my original intention when I invented this system and is in keeping with my stated intention when I offered it to the EAC to be used to conduct our elections back in 1990.

The licence agreement granted to the EAC states in article 6.1 as follows:-

"It is understood and agreed that the Licensee recognises and acknowledges that Ryan George Saunders Peralto is the inventor and owner of the Patents."

This clause was proposed by EAC member, Mr. Linton Walters, a lawyer and a nominee of Prime Minister P J. Patterson. It was unanimously supported by all members, as being representative of the facts and the history of this invention, as the records of the EAC clearly establishes. These records also recognize the fine tuning and adaptations the proposal went through, at the level of the committee and the EOJ, to satisfy in detail the special demands of the Jamaican electoral system.

After filing for the US Patent, I assured a colleague member of the EAC on our way to Parliament in 1996, that she could confidently expect that this invention could earn sufficient royalties which could provide all the funds needed to ensure educational opportunities in the future for every Jamaican if the royalty earned from its use is properly invested and managed. I expected this to begin to happen once all countries begin using it, in about ten years time, to ensure free and fair voting in their national elections.

This has been my position from the day I completed deciding on the design concept and began determining how to build the system and it will never change. I learned recently that it will require expert legal advice, vigilance and tenacity, to protect this Intellectual Property from being pirated and exploited by others, without any incremental benefit, beyond its use for Jamaican Elections, accruing to us as a people. I will begin to seek to rectify.

Valedictorian of the St. George's College graduating class of 1949, Ryan G. Peralto was all ears as the Reverend Father Charles Judah of the Society of Jesus delivers the main address.

President of Jaycees of Jamaica, JCI Senator, Ryan G. Peralto, makes a point to Jamaica's first native Governor General Sir Clifford Campbell at their Annual Convention 1970 as V. P. Keith Brown and a young Jaycees looks on.

First Vice President Ryan G. Peralto chairs the Jamaica Manufacturers Association export award function in 1974. Seated left to right Mrs. Sonia Vaz, the Hon. P. J. Patterson Minister of Trade and Industry, and Mr. Douglas Vaz JMA President.

The Mayor of Dade County, Florida, USA, Hon. Stephen Clarke with Senator Ryan G. Peralto, His Worship the Mayor of Kingston and St. Andrew, at the parade to celebrate the twinning of the two municipalities in 1981 in downtown Kingston.

Senator Ryan G. Peralto meets President Ronald Regan of the U. S. A., with Prime Minister Seaga at Jamaica House in 1981.

Senator Ryan G. Peralto meets President Nelson Mandela of South Africa during his official visit to Jamaica. Senator Oswald J. Harding looks on.

The agreement to bring the Caribbean Common Market into being is signed on behalf of Jamaica by the Minister of State responsible for Trade and Industry, the Honourable Ryan G. Peralto in Guyana, 1988. The Secretary General of the Caribbean Free Trade Association Roderick Rainford and his team look on.

Departure press conference in July 1992 held by the delegation from the Carter Center of Alanta, Georgia, USA, led by Senator Peralto to the elections in Guyana.

(Left - Right: David Carol, Dennis King, Senator Peralto, Guillermo Echavaria and Glenn Cowan)

Senator Ryan G. Peralto, Chairman of the Jamaica Labour Party, is introduced by Party Leader the Hon. Edward Seaga to the late Roman Catholic Pope, John Paul II during the official visit of the Pontif to Jamaica.

Senator Ryan G. Peralto hugs his dearest mother Muriel Peralto during her stay at his home in 2002.

Chapter Ten

WILL JAMAICA USE THIS INVENTION FOR VOTING?

Until the Electoral Commission is established by the Jamaican Parliament as successor to the EAC, I do not believe this will happen. As it stands now, it appears very unlikely that this system will be used for voting in elections in our nation in the immediate future. I vividly recall the EAC government member who told me emphatically in 1991 that this would not happen in my lifetime. He was supremely confident and as he is about to leave the political arena, he is looking more and more like an Elijah of Biblical fame.

Let us clinically examine where we have reached since May 1990 in trying to get a system in place capable of preventing the abuses that have plagued the Jamaican electoral process for so many years.

To evaluate the progress made in this direction I will now list the problems, the phase of the system which addresses each type of problem, and where Jamaica has reached in implementing the solution.

1. The Voters' List

Problems
a) The same elector is listed in more than one Polling Division or Constituency and is able to vote more than once in the same election.
b) The names of persons, who qualify and applied to be registered as electors, are accidentally or deliberately omitted from the Voters' List and so on election day, they are not permitted to vote.

c) Electors' names appear on the Voters' List for a Polling Division other than the one for the area in which they currently reside, and at which they expect to vote and are entitled to vote. On voting day, they cannot find the Polling Station where they are listed as an elector and so are unable to vote.

d) The names of persons who have died or have migrated are still on the official Voters' List, and other persons are allowed to vote in their names.

The Status

At least one **Fixed Centre** is in operation **in each constituency** and is managed by officials of the Electoral Office of Jamaica and officially monitored by representatives of the political parties recognized by the EAC to carry out:-

a) **Continuous Registration of electors**, by electronically recording their data inclusive of fingerprints and photographs.

b) Applications by **electors** for a **transfer** of their vote to **their new residence** are also recorded on the fixed centre equipment, and processed.

c) A **field team,** comprised similarly to the office team, visits the address supplied, for the purpose of **verifying the information provided.** The data is then sent to the central data processing department at the head office of the EOJ, along with supporting documentation from the field work .

The database of electors is continuously being upgraded and a new Voters' List is published twice per year, (end of May and end of November).

In the case of **an application for Registration as an elector or for a change of address, the new data once it is verified is then cross-matched** at the data processing department of the EOJ **against the data of every other person on the existing list of electors** who have all already been through that process.

If **no duplicate is found that person is added** to the working data base which is being compiled to produce the next Voters' List.

If a match is found among the existing list of persons on the Voters' List, then further field investigations are carried out, to determine if the applicant really needs a transfer or if an attempt is being made to establish a duplicate registration, and a decision made on how to treat that application, clerically and legally.

Report of the death of an elector is also investigated in the field and if the supporting information is obtained, then that person is **processed and removed from the list**.

In the case of an **elector who has migrated**, such a person **can only be excluded from** a new publication of **the Voters List if a re-verification exercise by a field team establishes that they are not currently and for the immediate previous six months been living in Jamaica.**

Note

a) A list of all proposed changes to be made to the list of electors, in order to publish and issue a new and up-to-date Voters' List is circulated to the political parties on a monthly basis. This enables the parties, to raise any objection or concerns and to have them discussed at the constituency meetings.

b) Monthly constituency meetings are held by each Returning Officer. Each political party is entitled to have representatives attend, to be kept up-to-date on all matters that affect the holding of elections and to try to agree on how to treat any issues raised.

c) A copy of the proposed new Voters' List is given to the political parties one month prior to publication. This is to allow time for any discrepancies to be settled before publication of the list, that is due at the end of May and November each year.

The **ERS** and the procedures employed in operating it have all been put in place and are being used very efficiently and effectively. Therefore, the problems with the Voters' List are being properly and effectively addressed.

2. Identification of Electors.

Problems

a) Improper identification, be it deliberate or accidental, permits persons to vote in the name of others.

b) Some bona fide electors whose names are on the Voters' List are denied identification and not allowed to vote.

The Status

The EVIBIS has been tested and it has performed excellently. It proved itself to be absolutely effective to deal with the above two situations of blatant fraud. Only a dishonest official can order the system to issue an official ballot to enable an impostor to vote. If that happens the equipment can tell you this was done and then the dishonest official can be penalized. The Constituted Authority if it so determines can nullify the balloting at that voting station and order new voting.

3. Securing the official Ballot Papers and protecting and counting the votes cast

Problems

a) Access to official ballot papers sometimes allows persons other than bona fide electors to cast votes and have them counted.

b) Access to marked ballots allows the opportunity for spoiling or stealing of properly marked ballots, which are then not counted.

The Status

The EVIBIS is not in place to prevent anything in # 3 from happening.
In the final analysis, the security safeguard for the system rests almost entirely on, the honesty, the goodwill, and the courage of the voting day officials, in each one of the nearly 7000 Polling Stations, and to a lesser extent on the Security Officers, especially as they cannot intervene inside a Polling Station unless invited in to do so by an election official.

Yes there some other mainly legal things that have been put in place, that should act as deterrents to persons, who wish to force a particular result of the voting at any polling place.

There are **Security Personnel** to prevent intimidation and interference with voters and to apprehend persons who abuse the process.

There is the "**Constituted Authority**" with its range of authority and power to suspend, stop, or abandon voting in any or all areas of the country, if it decides to do so for whatever reason, or to void the result of voting and declare the holding of new elections.

Then there is the "**Election Court**", with the power to impose any of the range of quite heavy fines, and punitive measures at its disposal, to deal expeditiously with any offenders or offences brought before it and proven.

IF JAMAICA FAILS TO IMPLEMENT THE "EVIBIS" ON AN ISLANDWIDE BASIS FOR THE NEXT ELECTION, FRAUDULENT VOTING WILL CONTINUE TO BE CARRIED OUT AND THE ELECTORAL SYSTEM WILL CONTINUE TO DESERVE TO BE CONDEMNED BY OUR PEOPLE ONCE THEY ARE GIVEN REASON TO DOUBT THE RESULT IN ANY VOTING STATION.

4. **Electors must be allowed to vote in private and in circumstances that are "free and fair and free from fear"**

Problems
   a) Crowds gather at Polling Station locations and intimidate electors into voting for a particular candidate.
   b) Electors are threatened by supporters to vote for a particular candidate and are required to show how they marked their ballot papers.

The Status
Nothing systemic and automated is in place to address the problems identified in #4, in order to avert, avoid, or prevent the spoiling or stealing of ballots. I am absolutely satisfied that the sure way to prevent those abuses lies in implementing Phase 3 of the system "Electronic Voting Jamaican Style" as agreed on by the EAC.

I believe the EAC members, who served with me up to May 2005, understand that Phase 3 really provides us with the best solution. Some of them have a reservation about using a fully automated system and the possibility of tampering with that process. I appreciate and understand their reservation.

I am not in any way concerned about that. The system can be made to reject any such attempt and identify if any such activity was tried. And let us also not forget, that the "Constituted Authority" has the power to abandon voting in such circumstances if it felt justified to do so.

To implement Phase 3 now, would really be taking far less risk than that which is currently being taken. Examine the opportunities provided at present for the result of an election to be rigged. Just add a few more constituencies to those that in the past have ignored and distorted the rules governing the process, and the proper operation of the system, and engaged in fraud and ballot rigging.

I do not find it difficult to believe that unsavoury elements, who have already infiltrated the political process and crave and would enjoy nothing better than to control state power or have more influence over those who have it, could decide to establish control over enough PD'S in selected constituencies and have votes cast to ensure the election of persons they wish to govern. Just examine the current social climate that prevails in our beloved Jamaica, with the level of corruption, lawlessness, and open defiance of constituted authority and then tell me that such a thing cannot happen.

If that happens as I am afraid it very soon may, it will be too late for talking and pleading. We shall simply be obliged and forced to take whatever steps are deemed necessary to restore to our people, our Constitutional Right to vote so that the majority of us can decide who shall be our leaders.

Many of our forefathers struggled and died to get us this far, in our quest for freedom, happiness, and prosperity and some of us are not prepared to give that up, not just so.

A closer look at the results of elections, in some constituencies should assist the reader to better appreciate why I came to conclusions, that caused me to have serious concerns and aroused my passion to develop and promote the use of Electronic Voting, to ensure it is the votes of the registered electors that determine who shall be the political leaders.

Parliamentary Elections 1989 (87 Of 60)	# P.Ds	# Voters on List	# P.Ds voted over 75%	# Voters in P.Ds over 75%	Votes Cast in P.Ds over 75%	Winner's Total in P.Ds over 75%	Loser's Total in P.Ds over 75%	Margin in P.Ds over 75%	Votes Cast in Const.	Winner's Total in Const.	Margin in Const.
St. Andrew											
East Central	91	19,502	47	8,415	8,407	7,276	1,131	6,145	15,608	11,276	7,188
North Central	66	16,810	27	4,910	4,969	3,152	1,817	1,335	12,242	7,017	1,873
Western	108	22,587	70	11,394	11,077	7,258	3,819	3,439	18,044	10,298	3,075
St. Mary											
South Eastern	95	17,683	77	11,359	11,304	6,254	5,050	1,204	13,869	7,319	843
St. Catherine											
Southern	88	21,220	53	8,835	8,775	4,805	3,970	835	16,276	8,325	474
East Central	93	19,961	47	7,131	7,095	5,124	1,971	3,153	14,902	9,744	4,674
Manchester											
Central	87	18,845	51	7,699	7,672	4,192	3,480	712	12,309	7,384	729

Statistical Data provided by the Electoral Office of Jamaica (EOJ)

Parliamentary Elections 1993 (7 of 60)	# P.Ds	# Voters on List	# P.Ds voted over 75%	# Voters in P.Ds over 75%	Votes Cast in P.Ds over 75%	Winner's Total in P.Ds over 75%	Loser's Total in P.Ds over 75%	Margin in P.Ds over 75%	Votes Cast in Const.	Winner's Total in Const.	Winner's Margin in Const.
Kingston											
East & Port Royal	95	15,625	53	8,929	8,823	8,518	305	8,213	11,643	10,683	9,714
St. Andrew											
North Central	57	13,004	4	919	915	609	306	303	7,635	3,903	171
South East	101	14,252	55	6,826	6,826	5,126	1,700	3,426			4,306
St. Mary											
South East	95	16,117	26	3,516	3,510	1,973	1,537	436	11,124	5,769	413
St. Ann											
South West	117	14,041	22		2,232	1,164	1,068	96	9,823	4,913	3
St. Catherine											
South Central	66	15,741	44	9,627	9,579	6,355	3,224	6,355	12,120	7,544	3,061
St. James											
East Central	80	12,813	25	2,855	1,703	1,523	207	1,316	8,803	4,617	330

Statistical Data provided by the Electoral Office of Jamaica (EOJ)

Parliamentary Elections 1993 (7 0f 60)	# P.Ds	# Voters on List	# P.Ds voted over 75%	# Voters in P.Ds over 75%	Votes Cast in P.Ds over 75%	Winner's Total in P.Ds over 75%	Loser's Total in P.Ds over 75%	Margin in P.Ds over 75%	Votes Cast in Const.	Winner's Total in Const.	Winner's Margin in Const.
St. Andrew											
Western	122	22,200	46	6,834	6,557	5,361	1,196	4,165	13,988	9,822	4,165
West Central	74	19,445	8	1,364	1,348	1,196	152	1,044	10,688	1,196	65
St. Ann											
South Western	118	16,121	75	8,493	8,176	4,628	3,548	1,080	12,716	6,363	614
St. Elizabeth											
South Western	93	19,023	73	12,870	12,716	6,763	5,953	810	15,406	7,956	710
St. James											
East Central	85	16,443	34	3,943	3,836	2,190	1,646	544	11,512	5,851	699
Clarendon											
North Western	129	18,640	73	8,880	8,190	4,874	3,316	1,558	13,407	5,943	204
St. Catherine											
South Central	88	21,614	36	6393	6,216	5828	388	5440	13,115	9,646	6,482

Statistical Data provided by the Electoral Office of Jamaica (EOJ)

Parliamentary Elections 2002 (4 of 60)	# P.Ds	# Voters on List	# P.Ds voted over 75%	# Voters in P.Ds over 75%	Votes Cast in P.Ds over 75%	Winner's Total in P.Ds over 75%	Loser's Total in P.Ds over 75%	Margin in P.Ds over 75%	Votes Cast in Const.	Winner's Total in Const.	Winner's Margin in Const.
St. Elizabeth											
South East	107	21,495	22	3,976	3,891	2,014	1,877	137	15,274	7,507	82
South West	93	21,365	25	4,716	3,925	2,056	1,869	187	15,298	7683	110
Portland											
Western	140	17,195	6	906	896	519	377	142	11,389	5,835	281
St. Mary											
South Eastern	106	18,910	8		1,483	847	602	245	12,305	6345	385

Statistical Data provided by the Electoral Office of Jamaica (EOJ)

This analysis of the most recent elections shows that there is still abnormally heavy and questionable voting taking place in selected areas, in certain constituencies, that results in one candidate winning by a margin that assures them of overall victory in the constituency. Improper and unfair practices in treating with important matters court violent reaction, which can result in national implosion and self destruction, as evidenced in our history. I hope we do not continue to journey along that road.

In the event that good sense does not soon prevail and the Jamaican Electronic Voting System installed, I pray that our Creator will guide the power seekers away from persisting rigging elections. This practice courts violent reaction and can result in national implosion and self destruction. Examples of such situations abound in our world, some quite close to our island home.

Jamaicans have a proud history of defying injustice. As a colony we had five notable slave uprisings. Our Maroons won a peace treaty from the British Empire, the most powerfull group of countries in the world at that time. Perhaps some of our present generation, or the next, may also have to die, to protect and preserve those rights and freedoms.

A view was put forward late in 2004 by Chairman Proffessor Errol L. Miller that the EVIBIS be used in selected constituencies. Mr. Abe Dabdoub and I did not share that view and said so. I proposed to the EAC that selection and training of persons to manage all Voting Stations begin in October 2005 in each parish, and a budget be put forward to finance full implementation of the EVIBIS for the election due in 2006.

If Phase 2, the EVIBIS, is not used nationally in the next election, impersonation and fraud will continue to take place in Voting Stations where it is not used. The abuses will be reported, offenders arrested, and the law will take its course.

No meaningful reform of the VOTING PROCESS would have taken place since the proposal of the new system was accepted

in 1990. Only the Elector Registration System would have been implemented after 15 years. If our populace does not begin to demand its implementation as a matter of urgency in no uncertain terms, I am beginning to feel that it may take us at least another 15 years and maybe never.

I believe as the time for an election draws closer, the Nation will be told that there was not enough time to recruit and train the cadre of persons required islandwide to operate what is a substantially an automated foolproof ballot issuing system. This argument will come from political quarters, as well as from others, who will get generous supporting media coverage to assist them to influence public opinion, and to hell with the wishes and Right of the majority of our people.

We will begin to hear arguments seeking to establish a pecking order of items on a National Agenda that have to be given priority at the expense of using the **EVIBIS** to identify each elector by fingerprint and issue one official ballot paper to each of them, which are the practical things the **EVIBIS** can do, plus produce a listing of electors identified and the number of ballots issued.

I hope that I will be proven incorrect in my analysis, but I am mindful that as a young nation we are still engaged in building in the hearts of all our people, loyalty, love and commitment to our democracy, and to our homeland Jamaica.

Many of us sing our National Anthem just mouthing the words. Most of us have not yet developed the commitment and willingness to make even the ultimate personal sacrifice, to protect the land of our birth. **We are not there yet but it will come one day.**

In the meantime, it makes good convenient political propaganda to proceed to blare out support for the new system to be implemented. **Our people, by and large, want a fair system to operate everywhere in Jamaica, and for all things.**

Talk of support for the new system is cheap and it impresses people when such statements are uttered. Some persons are deliberately given wide media exposure, when they make such statements to assist them, to gain public credence and confidence. Many such persons really have no commitment to seeing that the illegal practices are prevented, and later will be the ones making excuses for non implementation merely in an effort to soothe public concern.

The unfortunate truth is that Jamaica desperately needs leadership that possesses both the courage and the political will to put an end once and for all to stealing votes in an election, by putting the " Jamaican Designed Electronic Voting System " in place before we reach the point of no return.

We cannot afford for a lack of confidence and trust in the process and in the right of the persons who lay claim to have been elected to govern to again develop. This robs our nation of the confidence in, and support for, its elected leadership which are critical ingredients to spur us on to work together in nation building.

At the same time and of no less importance is a need to act rapidly, decisively, and effectively to remove from the fabric of our society the scourge of social indiscipline, and the lack of respect and rampant disregard displayed at all levels, for our laws, our values, and even the very lives of our people. I believe it is impatient of debate that both these things are of critical and of immediate importance, and demand decisive action, in order to restore stability and confidence in ourselves, and in the future we can build for our people in our land.

Social instability saps from a people their will and their energy to work assiduously to improve their quality of life. Invariably whenever such conditions obtain in Jamaica, our history tells us that too many of our trained people quickly move on and away to some foreign land. Many others who remain here, simply lapse into a survival mode. They make no significant effort to contribute to their own well being or to the national whole.

There is perhaps one third of native born Jamaicans living and working in other countries to support themselves and family members who live overseas and in our island. We, therefore, lose the direct effort of so many of our people to assist in building a better quality of life in our homeland.

It is important to remember, what history has tried to teach us. A country never dies. Its acceptability, its popularity, its importance to the human family, just fades. Unfortunately during that decline, invariably many of its people meet an untimely death, and inevitably, the memory of most of those, will also soon go away.

In a report dated 30 August 2004, Parliament was requested by the Electoral Advisory Committee to enact legislation to permit the use of the EVIBIS to conduct voting in national elections on an islandwide basis.

In March 2005, three Bills - viz. an Act to amend the Representation of the People Act, 2005, An Act to Amend the KSAC Act, 2005, and An Act to Amend the Parish Councils Act, 2005- were laid before Parliament, to create the legal foundation to allow its islandwide use to conduct voting.

During the debate in the Parliament on those Bills, the Honourable members of the Legislature took the opportunity to record sincere appreciation and thanks to those who served as members of the EAC over the 25 plus years since it was established.

The Parliamentarians who took part in that debate expressed high regard and respect for the work of the EAC viewing it as being very important to the preservation of our democracy. They felt that this committee had discharged its responsibility with distinction. Special commendation was offered in respect of the electronic processes that have been introduced over the last ten years, and the significant contribution this new approach has so far made, and can make to the integrity and acceptability of the results of elections held in Jamaica.

Chapter Eleven

THE HOUSE OF REPRESENTATIVES SPEAKS

The House of Representatives met on 1 March 2005 and considered the proposed Legislation, with the Honourable Speaker Mr. Michael Peart presiding.

Dr. the Honourable Minister Peter Phillips, Leader of Government Business, said this:-

"Mr. Speaker, the Bills -- I move first of all that the Bills, because of the similarity of the content, be debated simultaneously.

The Bills before us Mr. Speaker, significantly advance the process of electoral reform. And I think at the very outset Mr. Speaker, we can take note ,with pleasure, at the fact that whereas eight years ago the whole issue of electoral reform was front and centre in the public debate that by and large this issue does not command such central attention at the present time, and I think it is testament to the policy initiatives of this administration ,and indeed Mr. Speaker, to the common determination of both sides of the House to ensure that we have an electoral system, of such credibility and of such integrity, that not even the worst loser can complain that elections were not held freely and fair.

I think we should recall Mr. Speaker, some of the major reforms that have been undertaken. In 1994, I believe it was 1994,1995, the first of the major recommendations of the Electoral Advisory Committee on the legal reform of the electoral process was accepted by this House, which provided among other things, for the re-holding the nullification, and the voiding of elections in situations where there was violence of massive fraud, or compromising of the electoral process at any polling station or in any polling division or constituency and of course at around the same time, a new finger print based enumeration system was introduced.

These arrangements Mr. Speaker, have led us to the point where we are able to take yet another important step forward, and that is ,in the introduction of a ballot issuing system, an electronic identification and ballot issuing system, which is what these amendments will provide for:-

The introduction of Identification of electors by finger printing in the existing process of elector identification will assist in not only modernizing the electoral system but in aiding in minimizing the possibility of electoral fraud, by reducing, and hopefully eliminating the possibility of multiple voting and ensuring that the probability of impersonation is reduced.

Members of this House may recall that the Electoral Advisory Committee in its Report to Parliament dated August 30, 2004, recommended the introduction of a system of electronic identification of electors by fingerprinting in Parliamentary and Local Government elections throughout Jamaica.

This system was chosen after a series of demonstrations, followed by tests in two KSAC divisions in East St. Andrew in the parish Council elections held in June 2003. This new system will be used in areas to be designated by the EAC as it deems necessary. The general prerequisite of the system is that the elector is required to comply with the instructions of the presiding officer with respect to the fingerprint matching to determine identity and using the prescribed equipment in order for them to be issued with a ballot paper.

In this system the elector's live fingerprint will be matched with the fingerprint stored in the database that is maintained by the Electoral Office of Jamaica.

Once a match is made between the live fingerprint and the print in the Electoral Office's database the computer would generate a paper ballot which the elector will mark in secret and hand that ballot, in the same way as is normally done, to the presiding officer to be placed in the ballot box and then the electors, as is the case now, would dip their fingers in the electoral ink to ensure that they can be easily identified as an elector who has already voted.

If no matching fingerprint is found the elector would then be requested to answer questions generated by the computer from his demographic record contained in the database, which, along with the photograph would be used as an alternative identification procedure. So there is always an alternative procedure which is in place. Of course, if the elector satisfies neither procedure, then they will not be enabled to vote because it means that they would not have been properly registered.

The Bill retains the current procedures for the manual identification of electors. And these will apply in cases where the electronic voter identification system fails to function or fails to function properly.

With respect to the specific provisions of the Bill Mr. Speaker, the Representation of the People Act provides in clause 1 the short title of the proposed Act, namely, section 34 of the principal Act by deleting subsection(3) and substituting therefore a new subsection (3) and subsection (3A) to (3G),which sets out the procedures to be followed before the elector receives his ballot.

Pursuant to the proposed sub-section (3) the elector will not receive his ballot paper or be permitted to vote unless his identity is verified. The identity of the elector must be confirmed under the direction of the presiding officer or a duly authorized person in accordance with the procedural steps provided.

Subsection (3A) proposes that before receiving the ballot paper the presiding officer will direct the elector to place his finger on/ or the specified machine. Where a person refuses to have his identity verified by placing his finger on/ or in the specified machinery, subsection (3B) makes it clear that (a) ballot papers will not be issued and (b) erasing lines will be drawn through his name on the existing list of electors and in the poll book.

Subsection (3C) specifies that where the equipment fails to function or fails to function properly or no equipment is provided then the elector is to produce the identification card or other prescribed document which establishes his identity to the presiding officer, or, as the case may require satisfy the conditions specified at (7). Subject to the elector satisfying the conditions specified at (7), subsection (3B) provides that the presiding officer will only accept the prescribed document issued in substitution for an identification card.

In determining whether there is failure of equipment, subsection (3E) mandates-and that is important- that the presiding officer must seek and will be bound by the advice of the Chief Electoral Officer or his nominee. Clause 2(b) delete subsection (5) and (6) and substitute therefore new subsections (5) and (6). Subject to subsections (5) and (9) subsection (5) provides that where the elector fails to comply with (3B) no ballot paper will be issued and erasing lines will be drawn through his name on the official list of electors and in the poll book if also recorded there and the words 'refuse to be sworn' will be written thereafter.

Subsection (6) permits the candidates, their agents or any elector representing the candidate to examine the specified equipment as well as any document produced pursuant to subsection (3C) to establish an electors identity.

Clause (2)(c) delete certain words from subsection (7) of principal Act, clause (2) (d) inserts a new subsection (10) and defines the specified equipment as equipment approved by the EAC for the purpose of identifying electors by their fingerprint and issuing ballots". Similar provisions, Mr. Speaker have been inserted into section 50 of the KSAC Amendment Act, 2005 as well as in section 28 of the Parish Councils Act.

Mr. Speaker I think the amendments here are pretty straightforward. They follow the pattern that has already been applied and tested in previous Parish Council Elections and will now be made a provision of the Representation of the People Act on a permanent basis so that we will be able to apply electronic voter identification in subsequent elections to be held in Jamaican by-elections and general elections on the basis to be determined by the Electoral Advisory Committee. With these considerations, Mr. Speaker, I move second reading of the Bills".

Dr. Kenneth Baugh then Leader of the Parliamentary Opposition, made this presentation:-

"Mr. Speaker the Bill is not controversial, the three Bills before us today are not controversial concerning the Representation of the People Act, concerning the Parish Mr. Speaker,

I believe we ought to commend the work of those who have represented us as political parties and to commend the leadership of the Electoral Advisory Committee and we have the chairman here and members of the committee. And we want to commend all those who worked with them in the past and who are our present representatives, for having taken us to this tremendous achievement.

We should note that Jamaica is the first in the world to implement the application of electronic voter identification using fingerprint to ensure one man, one vote, same man, same vote". (Applause)

"As a matter of fact, Mr. Speaker, I have learnt that the same contractor is employed presently — that Cogent Systems Limited — is employed in implementing in the United States of America using fingerprint ID and of course Mr. Speaker, more sophisticated technology is being used by the United States of America for the purpose of immigration and building up a database concerning immigrants.

Mr. Speaker, this obviously contributes to the consolidation of our democratic ideal and is an effort to eradicate corruption at the polls. No Jamaican who has experienced elections over the last twenty to thirty years can deny the fact that in the past contaminated political processes by extension have infected several levels of public administration and today we have the unfortunate rank of being among the most corrupted countries.

I once had a principal of my old school, Cornwall College, who said to students constantly, that slackness in one department, any department of life inevitably leads to slackness in all departments of life. Clearly implying, Mr. Speaker, that the character of any institution and the character of a nation is determined by its leadership, which sets the terms of reference, the frame of reference and sets the paradigm in which others operate, in which others take their cue. And, therefore, this new measure will help to assist to eradicate not only corruption at the polls on the day of election but help to eradicate intimidation or any other means of influencing the voter.

I say not completely, Mr. Speaker, because there is no question that there will still be efforts and we still have work to do to make sure that people feel free to express their political will without coercion, without undue influence.

The system, Mr. Speaker, was implemented in Eastern St. Andrew for the Parish Council elections, and those who know report to us that it was ninety-eight percent effective in what it set out to do. It is now set for island wide implementation and it is intended to be used in the by-election in West Kingston.

And Mr. Speaker, I have to admit that the Prime Minister has acted in good faith having committed himself to ensuring that this Bill comes to the House to be taken through all stages". **(Applause)**

"I'm certain, Mr. Speaker, that the outcome of the implementation of this electronic voting will prove to both sides of the House and to the country that the overwhelming sympathies of the West Kingston electorate is for rights and justice and tangible improvements to the quality of their lives and their wellbeing.

There is no question, Mr. Speaker, that post-election concerns have led to a number of initiatives through dialogue, in establishing and in the evaluation of the Electoral Advisory Committee soon to be considered to be an electoral commission and also for establishing the constituted authority for rapid decision making concerning the outcome of elections.

Later concerns, Mr. Speaker, I'm certain from both sides of the House, the country will hear from us that we are considering funding for political campaign and funding for political activity to preserve democracy and to protect democracy from the onslaught of big money and the misuse of resources, public resources by incumbents to political advantage.

Mr. Speaker, we have all to welcome the advent of this event because it indicates very clearly that we have the moral commitment to ethics for the sake of ethics itself and for the sake of goodwill and basic principles. Mr. Speaker, this is a step in the right direction and we have no hesitation whatsoever, in giving our full support to the three Bills before the House today. Thank you very much". **(Applause)**

Mr. Delroy Chuck made the following statement:-

"Mr. Speaker, I would just like to add my support and in particular to congratulate the members of the Electoral Advisory Commission who have worked assiduously to make sure that electronic voting is coming into being step by step". **(Applause)**

"If this works well, Mr. Speaker, one hopes that at a general election we can have similar electronic voting, even though we still have major steps to take to have fully implemented electronic voting. As you are aware, Mr. Speaker, this is merely identification of the voters.

But, Mr. Speaker , I think the stage should be set where persons in the country can vote not only at particular polling stations, but once they reside in a particular area they can vote anywhere in the country. Unfortunately, Mr. Speaker, there are still many persons who are very fearful of going out to vote on election day.

And we must avoid that situation so that whether they are in the supermarket, whether they are in the pharmacy once there is some form of internet kiosk available they should be able to put in the necessary information, perhaps even with an ID a fingerprint identification and vote.

Even from home, because, Mr. Speaker, I say this, technology is moving very rapidly. When we see, Mr. Speaker, the technology which is available even to us here in Jamaica that we can pay our bills sitting at home, we can pay all the JPS, NWC all the bills sitting at home passing thousands, sometimes millions of dollars, Mr. Speaker, via the internet or electronic voting, there is no reason why we should not go the further step where at election time we should be able to vote electronically.

In support, Mr. Speaker, of the Bill may I say that it has been reported that I said that there won't be any talks on the Constitution until there is an election in West Kingston. How could I have said that, Mr. Speaker, save and except to say that certainly there have been many talks between the Minister of Justice and myself on the Constitution.

All that we were looking at is a time period, Mr. Speaker, and now that the Bill will be passed today we hope it will get to the Senate this week, and hopefully by the weekend or early next week the Prime Minister's hands will be free to call the election". **(Applause)** *"and we urge him, Mr. Speaker, to exercise his freedom as quickly as possible".*

Mr. Abraham Dabdoub said the following:-

"Thank you very much, Mr. Speaker.

Mr. Speaker, I rise to support this Bill and to say to this Honourable House that we have come a very long way since 1979.

Because it was in 1979 that the Electoral Advisory Committee was set up and I believe the Most Honourable Prime Minister had something to do with it, as did I and the former Leader of the Opposition who is no longer with us.

I also must say, sir, that I think this must be very pleasing to my friend, the Minister Honourable Paul Robertson, because from the moment we first sat on the committee we thought of how we could use fingerprints but the technology was not then available.

I believe also that it is appropriate to pay commendation to a former colleague of this House and the Senate, Senator Ryan Peralto". (Applause) " who has been very instrumental in the conceptualizing of different types of technology to come together to give us what we have today.

Mr. Speaker, I think the Electoral Advisory Committee, soon to become a Commission, all the members who serve especially the selected members, ought to feel good today and be congratulated for bringing the matter to the point where we now have an electronic or what I would call a semi-electronic system of voting which will ensure one man, one vote, same man, same vote. Unless of course, we get to the stage where people might wish to do things to other people, which I hope we will never get.

So, Mr. Speaker, let me say, these Bills are perhaps the first step towards a complete electronic voting system, although I don't join with my friend in saying that we will never reach the stage where we will vote by internet. But I certainly can visualize the stage where we can vote by touching a screen and having the vote recorded. Because as the society becomes more sophisticated that they will learn to accept what exists in other countries, pure electronic voting.

We have gone this route, Mr. Speaker, because to jump to a purely electronic system would be to forget the culture of our people who like to see what they are doing and make the mark for the representative of their choice by looking and seeing that it is marked beside the bell or beside the head as the case may be.

So, Mr. Speaker, let me say it is appropriate I think, given the history of where we are coming from and the fight for electoral reform, that the first time it will be used in an election for parliamentary seat will be in the constituency of the former Member of Parliament for West Kingston the Most Honourable Edward Seaga, and I am sure he himself would be pleased. Thank you very much Mr. Speaker". **(Applause)**

Dr. St. Aubyn Bartlett made the following presentation:-

"Thank you Mr. Speaker. Mr. Speaker, I rise to give support to these Bills, and indeed to give testimony to the effectiveness of this system because it is a system which was tested in my own constituency.

Mr. Speaker, I wish to commend the former Leader of our great party and also a former Senator, Ryan Peralto, and especially to Mr. Peralto for insisting that voters could be identified by finger prints and that by that mechanism we could also trigger a ballot.

When others thought it could not happen, Mr. Peralto insisted that it could happen.

And, Mr. Speaker, who is better to have been the Chairman of the Electoral Advisory Commission to see this dream come alive, but Professor Miller, who himself was denied on an occasion when he went to vote because there were other people who were there impersonating the voter and when I spoke to him on an occasion I know that he was committed to ensuring that we would have a system in this country where we can have one man, one vote, same man, same vote. (Applause) So that when the Professor goes to make his vote he knows that nobody can make that vote, except him.

I must say that the use of the system in my own constituency was for the identification of the voters and I am happy to hear that there is now an added dimension to the system because the use of the finger print will not only identify the voter but it will also assist in triggering the ballot.

Because in my constituency though it went well, because it did not trigger a ballot, there were instances in which there were one and two events that needed to be checked into properly. And I am sure that with the addition to the system now whereby the finger print will trigger the ballot that we will get rid of any of the little chicanery that can be associated with just identifying the voter.

And so, Mr. Speaker, it is my pleasure to commend the system and to hope that when it is used in Western Kingston we will see once and for all that this is the best system for voting in Jamaica and that the world will copy Jamaica and have this system in place. I thank you very much". (Applause)

Mr. Michael Henry had this to say:-

"Mr. Speaker, much as I share all the joy that I hear, I share some sorrow because this reflects that where there is a will there is a way and I find it very unfortunate that in a country that we have, that we find it so quick to finger print people for the process for which the political system needs them. But we have languishing on the House of Parliament, the National Registration Bill to register all our citizens in this country for which I think it is more important than merely for voting. And this kind of action sends the message that we need the people only for three or four areas of their life.

And I am therefore, using this to appeal to the Government and by extension, the Ministry where it lies, that we revive very quickly the national registration of our citizens, that we ensure they are provided with a social security number and that TRN is when you have a business, you see, we only need the people when they go to school and we don't finger print them then but when we need to tax them with the TRN and when we need them to vote.

And since we have thousands of people unemployed and thousands who don't vote we continue to perpetuate these numbers which really have no relevance in reality.

And since, part of the thing that is holding up the Bill is that I have insisted that the fathers be finger printed and put on the birth certificates I believe that we must revive the Bill, if that is the only thing holding it up I think we can overcome it.

But I do believe it is important for this country to have a national registration of all its citizens and to extend that to the wide body of everyone who lives in this country and is born in this country. And I trust today's joy which is important in the development process will lead us to taking it to the next step of reviving that Bill and making sure it gets through this House. Thank you very much, Mr. Speaker".

Dr. the Honourable Peter Phillips then wound up this debate:-

"Mr. Speaker, I am very pleased for the extensive support from that side for the Bills. Indeed, Mr. Speaker, I would like also, Mr. Speaker, to join in commending the Electoral Advisory Committee both the current members and members past, for the work that they have done in this regard. **(Applause)**

And I would certainly want to recognize in particular at this point the work done by Professor Gladstone Mills in having" **(Applause)** *"pioneered the development of the system and of the concept.*

You know, Mr. Speaker, when I think of the numbers of persons from whence this deliberation came there are persons including the Honourable Paul Robertson, other members of the committee over the period included, Portia Simpson Miller, O.K. Melhado, D. K. Duncan, myself, Maxine Henry-Wilson, Donald Buchanan, Burchell Whiteman, Linton Walters, on occasions I know Karl Samuda was a member of the committee, Anthony Johnson, Bartlett and others as well as Senator Ryan Peralto and a number of others. And indeed there have been a number of other independent members. It has been long in the making. But I also think it is important to note, Mr. Speaker, and I want to mention this, I think it is important to note that there have been other significant amendments.

The process of getting a credible, acceptable internationally recognized system of free and fair elections hasn't just resulted from the use of technologies.

We must bear in mind and I think some of the most far-reaching proposals inspired in the main by the contribution by the Most Honourable Prime Minister, resulted in the legal reforms coming before the Electoral Advisory Committee and accepted by this House which provided for the voiding of elections by the constituted authority where there are widespread breaches. And I think that that bit of legislation has at least concentrated the minds of those who use to conspire to distort elections in the past.

And I would also in this regard want to sound a note of caution against those who say we must just move willy nilly to electronic voting. Let me say that in jurisdictions some of them not too far from us, the experience of electronic voting has not been free from mal-practice. Ask voters in many States in the United States who have had concerns, in Ohio and in Florida and elsewhere. So I think we have a good system and what is important is that it has been devised by Jamaicans for Jamaica and for Jamaican conditions". **(Applause)**

"I want also, Mr. Speaker, especially as we are envisaging by-elections and the call for by-elections and the timing. I want to make a general point. Free and fair elections is not just a matter of what system you have in place on the day. There is a question of the kind of practices, the democratic practices of the contenders, the candidates in an election and of their party supporters.

I would hope that we are able and everybody has an opportunity to show it, some will be able to show it very soon that scrutineers and canvassers will be free to go into every community in their constituencies". **(Applause)**

"And that, gone will be the days and may they be far gone when candidates have to turn up at a nominating centre in an armoured car because they are not permitted to travel freely in the country". **(Applause)**

"So anybody can come and walk anywhere, anywhere, anytime, any hour of day". **(Applause)**

"Seriously let me say, we need to get to that point. You know there have been polls done and studies done of the young people and when you ask them their concept of what an election is in some communities they see it as a time of mayhem, of violence and of animosity one Jamaican towards another. Let us take this as the start, not the end of something. **(Sotto voce comment)**

Yes Bustamante Highway, PNP must keep a meeting there without problems, Coronation Market. In fact, we used to keep meetings at Coronation Market when the rod of correction was unveiled, and you will remember, those days, you were PNP, **(Laughter)** *and you may be again, all right.*

But, Mr. Speaker, quite seriously, democratic practice filtering through down to every indoor agent and outdoor agent and every runner is an important complement to this system that we are instituting here.

Mr. Speaker, I am pleased to hear the support for the National Registration Bill and I think that for all kinds of reasons I have heard the support in this House, I have heard it voiced elsewhere, and I think it is good that we can now hopefully reinvigorate the proceedings of the committee which is considering this.

Mr. Speaker, I think the Bills before us do credit to the commonality of purpose and to the determination of both sides to have a system of elections which is a credit to the entire Jamaica and to our reputation as a country. And so, Mr. Speaker, I move second reading of these Bills".

The Honourable Speaker: -
The House will now resolve itself into a committee of the whole House to consider these Bills clause by clause.-

COMMITTEE STAGE
Dr. the Honourable Peter Phillips:-
"Mr. Chairman, I am proposing that we, in the case of - we take each Bill separately, Mr. Chairman, and I am proposing that we take them en bloc they having been considered and given that there is no amendment being proposed here, Mr. Chairman".

RESUMPTION
The Honourable Speaker:-
"I do report these three Bills, An Act to Amend the Parish Councils Act, An Act to Amend the Kingston and St. Andrew Corporation Act and An Act to Amend the Representation of the People Act, having passed Committee Stage without amendment".

Dr. the Honourable Peter Phillips:-
" Mr. Speaker, I move for third reading of the Bills".

The Honourable Speaker:-
"The question is for third reading of the Bills".
(Motion put to the House and agreed to)

Dr. the Honourable Peter Phillips: -
"Mr. Speaker, before moving on to the next".

The Honourable Speaker:-
"Minister Phillips one minute, Minister Phillips.

A Bill entitled, **"AN ACT to Amend the Representation of the People Act,"** *read a third time and passed.*

A Bill entitled, **"AN ACT to Amend the Kingston and St. Andrew Corporation Act,"** *read a third time and passed.*

And a Bill entitled **"An act to amend the Parish Councils Act",** *read a third time and passed."*

Chapter Twelve

THE SENATE TAKES A POSITION

The Senate met on 11 March 2005, and considered the Bills, with the Honourable President Mrs. Syringa Marshall – Burnett, CD- presiding.

Senator the Honourable Minister Burchell Whiteman, the Leader of Government Business had this to say:-

"Madam President, we propose to take the items listed at numbers 1, 2 and 3 on the Order Paper. Following well established practice, we do not expect to have a divide on these particular Bills, but we never know. But I would like Madam President, to start with some procedural points which I hope we will all agree. The three Bills have a great deal in common, the Memorandum of Objects and Reasons in each case is virtually identical in wording. The differences in the Bill relate to references in clause 2, section 34 of ROPA, Section 28, Representation of the People Act. Clause 2 also refers to section 28 of the Parish Councils Act and section 50 of the KSAC, Kingston and St. Andrew Corporation Act.

That is the essential difference, the substance is the same. All three Bills, Madam President, will have clause by clause consideration at Committee Stage. But I just want to indicate that my contribution to the debate in moving these motions, except at Committee Stage, will be made in one presentation, which I am now about to do.

I intend to move an amendment, as requested by the Leader of the House of Representatives, in response to concerns raised in that Chamber and I want to make it clear that he and I are responding to concerns which I know the Electoral Advisory Committee had, notwithstanding the consultations which took place prior to the tabling of the Bill. They are legitimate concerns because it is important to get the system right. So I don't want anybody to go around saying that this amendment was moved to delay any processes. It happened in the Lower House and we were simply taking it now.

These Bills, Madam President, represent a significant and very positive departure from long established practices and therefore we must, as legislators, ensure that what we are about to

113

do is correct, that what we are about to do is accepted by the decision makers, is in the interest of the Jamaican people, is sustainable, and most important, allows for the democratic will of the people to be exercised without successful legal challenge to any aspect of what we prescribe. I know that my opposite number on that side is very particular on these matters.

It says you don't legislate for who is in office at any particular time, you want the law to ensure that what is there protects the citizens of the country, protects those to whom it applies. And so this amendment is what you might even say, is a last minute amendment, is to ensure that what is done really represents the correct procedure when it comes to the day of voting and reflects what accords with existing practice, what you might call the sort of fallback position when a voter comes to be identified.

I am going to read the proposed amendment now, and it is this, that in clause 2 - I am doing it to put into the record the amendment which is coming before us.

What is being proposed in clause 2 of each of the Bills, that we replace 3(c) by the following wording:-

"Where the specified equipment fails to function, or to function properly, or no such equipment is provided the elector shall-

(a) produce to the presiding officer his identification card or other prescribed document establishing his identity; and

(b) take the oath in the form set out in the Second Schedule and otherwise establish his identity to the satisfaction of the presiding officer; or

(c) as the case may require, satisfy all the conditions specified in subsection (7)."I will read it again,

"Where the specified equipment fails to function, or to function properly, or no such equipment is provided the elector shall-

(a) produce to the presiding officer his identification card or other prescribed document establishing his identity; and

(b) take the oath in the form set out in the Second Schedule and otherwise establish his identity to the satisfaction of the presiding officer; or

(c) as the case may require, satisfy all the conditions specified in subsection (7)."

When you look at subsection (7) and you look at what was in the original Bill, or the Bill that is before us in its present form, you will see, Madam President, that there is not a very great deal of difference but this wording has been proposed to ensure that what we do is consistent as a default position, a fall back position with what now obtains; that you are not asking the elector to do any more or any less to prove that he is the person deserving of that ballot or entitled to that ballot than existed before.

And may I, at this point, restate something, Madam President, which has been said many times but which does not seem to be fully appreciated or understood. The legislation we are about to pass does not address electronic voting. We are not about to introduce electronic voting in Jamaica.

The experience elsewhere has not filled us, at least certainly has not filled me, with any degree of confidence in systems of electronic voting.

What we are about is the full scale introduction of electronic voter identification for the purposes of giving the elector, the registered elector, a ballot to which he is entitled and to give that ballot to nobody else who may claim to be that registered voter. One person, one vote. The registered person listed in that polling division, his or her ballot paper.

This is not about electronic voting. It is about identifying a person by his previously registered fingerprints as the person with that name, with the declared antecedents, mother, grandmother, whatever, belonging to that polling division and, therefore, enabling him or her to generate his or her own ballot paper without refusal. Indeed, Madam President, we are empowering the genuine voter.

The acronym being used for this system the **EVIBIS**, *Electronic Voter Identification and Ballot Issuing System. The voter is identified by fingerprint using this system, the computer system, the electronic system and that triggers the release of the ballot to him or her.*

The amendment we take this morning makes provision for the alternative means of identification if the equipment fails. And I will at a later stage, if needed, address the issue of the likelihood of failure, which is actually very slim.

But, Madam President, I would like us to locate this Bill and its consequences in the historical development of the electoral system of Jamaica.

We have come a very long way and I think we should be very proud of just how far we have come. " **(Applause)**

"We are now, and have been for some time, a model and a resource for other countries in the region and beyond. I am resisting the temptation to call names, for very good reasons.

But it cannot be denied, Madam President that we have passed through some experiences which we are very happy to put behind us.

At the risk of offending the ladies, I recall one occasion in the 1960s when the shape of a particular constituency, as drawn by the architect of the system at that time, prompted the late Michael Manley to describe its phallic character, which bore no relation to the community of interest which constituency boundaries were intended to protect and preserve.

And, Madam President, I would be less than honest if I suggested that gerrymandering or redistricting, as it is called in some other jurisdictions, was the preserve of one political party.

The fact is that since 1979, with the creation of the Electoral Advisory Committee there has been steady, though not all together linear progress in developing a system which harnesses the best of what political leadership brings to the table and curbs the excesses to which political control is likely to lead.

Perhaps the most important developments in the process have taken place within the last ten or twelve years — *I think we have an electronic problem somewhere".*

Senator the Honourable A .J. Nicholson:-

"Use the alternative".

Senator the Honourable Burchell Whiteman continued:-

Perhaps, as I said the most important developments have taken place in the last ten or twelve years and the ultimate step will be taken, I think, when as is coming before this Parliament at some stage and I hope sooner rather than later, the Bill to create and establish an Electoral Commission, which will be ultimately entrenched.

As we stand today, all things being equal, perhaps they are not, as we stand today, Madam President, the Electoral Advisory Committee is composed of selected and nominated members and it constitutes a model which has worked and worked well. Three persons of good repute and high level of acceptability, selected by the Governor General and two persons from the political parties, one from each major political party with alternates named by the political parties. It has built confidence in the system.

The EAC operates using a consensual approach. **And I am very happy that my colleague, who is still called Senator Ryan Peralto in those quarters, is here this morning to be a party to what we are doing.** (Applause) **There have been important reforms over the period; reforms in the area of enumeration and registration of voters; reforms in the preparation and publication of the National Voters List.**

I think some of us can remember the days when the list would come out a couple days before election - general administration of the electoral system; the polling procedures, including voter identification and other legal reforms including that which provides for a constituted authority which can deal with matters of the voiding of poll by virtue of being in position on election day to deal with matters as they arise. So there have been very signifi-

cant reforms, Madam President, and I just want to touch briefly on some of them.

First of all, and I think perhaps the most important one, in terms of registration of voters. In 1996 the Representation of the People Act was amended to provide for the establishment of fixed registration centres. The system was piloted in two constituencies, one in the Corporate Area and one outside.

And after that it was implemented nationally with the result that electors had the option of visiting a fixed centre at any time, they did not have to wait on an enumeration period, a house to house enumeration period. They could visit an electoral office, a registration centre at any time and have themselves registered, subject to various other processes of checking and residence verification, have themselves registered as a voter.

Following a pilot exercise in 1996, during the full enumeration in 1997, the fingerprints of all electors were collected along with their photographs and demographic data. And the most important feature of the new system was its ability to cross-match the fingerprints of electors in order to duplicate and, therefore, be able to remove duplicate registration; to detect and remove the duplicate registrations.

And then, Madam President, following the production of the 1997 voters list, the enumeration process became a continuous one where eligible persons not yet on the voters list could visit a fixed registration centre within their constituency at any time and have their names added to the electoral list. Arrangements have been made, the system is in place to deal with people who change their address and what all this has done is make the system much more user-friendly for those who wish to exercise their democratic right to vote.

In terms of the voters list, Madam President, the system also provides for a new voters list to be published every six months and the six-month periods are fixed, end of November and we are coming up now - well the March period is coming to a close, hence a rush on the Electoral Office and at the end of March that will be a cut off and another voters list will be generated.

This allows for good order. It is now known to all and sundry when voters list will be closed and published, that is to say the process for arriving at the voters list is closed and published. Registration continues, 1st of April it continues but then those persons would not appear on a list until the list is closed off in November. And so it goes on.

So, Madam President, as I said we have come a long way and there is now much more confidence in the system and what we are seeking to do is to ensure that there is more understanding of how the system works and that it works in the interest of the electors.

There are some other administrative things. For example, Election Day workers can now vote prior to Election Day so that they are free, without any stress to do their duties on Election Day.

The Constituted Authority, as I said, was brought into being. The Constituted Authority is chaired by a retired Puisne Judge and it comprises a Privy Councillor and three selected members of the Electoral Advisory Committee. They monitor Election Day proceedings from a central point. They receive reports from each constituency, each division; they are empowered to collect evidence on election day malpractices and recommend to the Election Court the halting or voiding of the polls, either in a single or group of polling stations effectively necessitating a retaking of the poll in the affected areas.

So all these things I bring to attention to remind ourselves of the changes, reforms which have taken place to the benefit of the system.

Now, we are dealing with technology about which people always have concerns. There are very careful systems in place — and I know Senator Peralto is extremely strong on this point — to ensure the integrity of the use of the technology. *It is not a case that all and sundry have access to critical data or to critical systems, so what we have is a foolproof — well, I shouldn't say foolproof because every time we think we have a foolproof system, there comes a Jamaican who can beat it, and we are a very creative people. We have a system of integrity and we have a system which allows us to have confidence in the results of any election.*

Not only do we have computers at the registration centres which are able to take the data and to have instant transmittal to the centre, but at the centre we have high-speed computers capable of cross matching the fingerprints of each elector with all other electors in the database in a relatively short time. So we can get virtually instant checks as to whether elector A in Hanover is really different from somebody by the same name of elector B over in St. Thomas, and that is the level to which we have reached.

And moreover, the genuine elector who is issued with an identification card, gets a card now which is produced by a very powerful machine, a very effective card, which is very much in demand and is used by voters for a variety of purposes, and of course all of them honourable, to establish their identification.

Madam President, this legislature as constituted now and in the past, has been responsible for making many changes to the law to ensure that the system that we have in place is one that serves us well. We have amended the law to allow for the registration in fixed centres, for the process of enumeration to be a continuous one, for no election to be held on a voters' list which is more than six months old and so a list has to be published every six months.

We have laws which allow us to monitor the movement of candidates on election day to provide for certain restrictions, we have laws which have increased the penalties for electoral malpractices and we have new offences with sanctions including the offence of duplicate registration. And as I said, we have the Constituted Authority.

This particular exercise in which we are engaged this morning is to facilitate the use of the voter identification electronic voter identification system. I will just remind, Madam President, that in the 2003 - in the 2002, 2003, sorry, KSAC Local Government Election, provision was made for a pilot to be conducted in two divisions in the constituency of St. Andrew Eastern. A pilot was carried out in the Mona division of the constituency and again the law allowed for a reversion to the manual process if the system failed.

My understanding is, and I think my recollection is correct, that there was a ninety-eight per cent success in the use of the equipment in those two divisions and what we are doing now is seeking to establish this as the standard means by which people will vote on election day across the country, whether it be in a Local Government election, in a general election, by-election, any election held under the laws of Jamaica will now be done on this basis.

Again, I want to say that we are not about electronic voting, we are about electronic voter identification, again using the basic system, a person's fingerprints, bio-data, all of which are fed into the system and which provide for corroboration at the time of election by electronic means. And it is in that spirit, or it is with that intention and in the confidence that what we are doing here is advancing our electoral process one step further and therefore deepening the democratic systems which allow us to do what we do as a country that I invite my colleagues to give very favourable consideration to all three of these Bills.

So, Madam President, as we can see the Bill essentially has two clauses, the short title and construction and in the second clause in each case you have the Act being amended to ensure that the voter is identified by means of the electronic system. There are deletions and substitutions and the basic point of the substitution is that no elector will receive and be permitted to vote unless he has fulfilled the conditions provided for, which is that he follows the instructions of the presiding officer, puts his finger on the machine, has himself or herself identified and the ballot paper is issued in that way.

If it fails to function then the default position kicks in and he identifies himself to the satisfaction of the presiding officer and is sworn or affirms that he is the elector. That is checked and he is allowed to vote.

So those, Madam President, are the few remarks which I wish to use to introduce the Bill and as I say, I invite my colleagues to support the Bill". **(Applause)**

Opposition Senator:-

"One week late".

Government Senator:-
"Never too late, for a shower of rain".

Senator the Honourable A.J. Nicholson:-
"No man, no man, take out the shower business". **(Laughter)**

Senator Anthony Johnson, the Leader of Opposition Business had this to say:-
"Madam President, let me say I don't accept that there is well-established precedent about taking three Bills and reading them as one. I don't believe in the system. You could kill me dead. I don't believe in it. I don't think it is right. And you are using an opportunity when you know that there is a compulsion on all of us to ensure that the spirit of the Representation of the People Act is carried through.......(**Cross talk**)*...and that we have....*

Now, what has happened is that the Minister has given us a view on how the system has been proceeding and I would like to join with him in saying that we have come a far way. The process as developed by the Electoral Advisory Committee which was done in the early 1990s when I had the honour to be a member, is that we had a three-stage process was to identify and test methods of electronic identification and to have a pilot. At that we would determine whether the system was worth further work, whether we would move ahead along those lines.

That process has been completed with remarkable success despite nay sayers, negative types, people who are not interested in new technology and above all people who wanted to keep the system corrupt. (Sotto voce comments)

We now move to — I speak with feeling, I speak with feeling as one who has had to take very serious decisions not to be a thief. Because I don't believe you can be a thief — the country can't succeed if you steal. And you cannot have a system that is based on people who steal. Now that's a fact.

The second stage, which we are now about to enter, is to have identification island-wide. I don't know in fact if there is any other country which has a nation-wide system of electronic identification and the fact that we have been able to work on it and work on it so fast and to get it working is in very large part due to the tremendous amount of application and dedication of the members of the Electoral

Advisory Committee and in particular the member who took it on himself to do a lot of the technical work, Senator Ryan Peralto, who is with us here this morning". (Applause)

"But, Madam President, it was never intended to be the end of the process. The third stage was to have been and is to be electronic voting, because there are many countries in the world that have electronic voting. That is not peculiar to Jamaica.

The process of electronic voting in other parts of the world, however, is not from a point of view of assisting identification or cutting down rascality, bogus voting, mass voting and so on.

The process is to speedily vote and record which electronic methods are quicker than manual methods. But that really has not been our real problem. Our problem is the identification and ensuring one man, one vote".

Senator the Honorable A.J. Nicholson:-
"That's right".

Senator Anthony Johnson continued:-
Same man, same vote, voting free and fair and free from fear." Those were the three elements which we used and we have been using for some time to indicate the pathway on which we propose to proceed.

So the Leader of Government Business has said that he is not satisfied that electronic voting is sound, that it is necessarily the way to go. I can advise him that I suspect that he is the victim of a tremendous propaganda campaign in a recent election in a nearby country where persons expected one candidate to win.

The candidate didn't win and so they claimed that it was because they corrupted the electronic voting system.

Let us say that the systems of electronic voting are extremely well developed, they understand the back room how it works, there are checks and balances, and if any such defalcations or whatever have occurred they have means of checking them despite what you hear people saying. But they have means of checking them. And in the larger countries certainly for instance India, that had its elections within the last few months and they were able to complete the voting electronically.

They were able to complete it in a very short space of time and they had no reports of any infractions of the system and they had a voters' list of somewhere over three hundred million people. So we are moving ahead on good grounds and we are moving ahead in a fair way. And I hope that we will continue at this path.

Madam President, it is not a secret that this particular provision in three Bills the Representation of the People Act, the Kingston and St. Andrew Corporation Act and the Parish Councils Act is being done because of a need to improve the system but also because it has been stated by the Head of the Government that he would like to have that completed before a certain by-election is called. Now, I don't know why.

I would like to say however, that in the case at hand the Member of Parliament resigned on the 19th of January, this year. Today is the 11th of March and within seven days time it will be a full three months. And I would submit, I would submit ... **(Sotto voce comment.)**

I would submit, I would submit that - it's two months - **(Laughter)** *I would submit that there have been by-elections that have been held at much longer intervals and by-elections that have been held at much shorter intervals.*

It might interest you to know Madam, that on the 7th of November 1993, the existing Prime Minister announced that a member intended to resign and that a new member had been proposed.

And so on the 9th of November Mr. Hartley Jones, known familiarly to us as Bobby, resigned as the Member for South St. Andrew. When he resigned on the 9th the nomination day was the 13th, a few days after. The election was the 30th.

So between the time that the Prime Minister made his announcement of what was to happen and the election was less than a month. Between the time of Nomination Day and the election was the expected 16 days and between the resignation and the election was 21 days, 21 days. **(Sotto voce comments)**

There is no reason ... **(Sotto voce comments)** *There was no reason for any delay. As a matter of fact, Madam, the interesting thing about it, the interesting thing about it, is that that particular constituency has a common border with the constituency which is now being considered. Same type of people,* **(Laughter)** *same area within indeed a stone's throw from us as we speak in this hallowed Chamber.*

So we look and listen and we expect that there will be adequate notice of this precedent and of the fact that it is not good to have people without political representation at any time. And the extent to which there is a reduction of the time that people are without representation would put us in the area of something to be proud, of which the Leader of Government Business spoke so feelingly a while ago.

Madam President, these Bills have been the subject of intensive review and discussion by the members of the Electoral Advisory Committee and we have gone through them in our respective parties, they have laid on the Table for the last week. The Opposition has no objection to any of the clauses that are included therein".

Senator the Honourable Burchell Whiteman:-
"In the first Bill."

Senator Anthony Johnson continued:-
"Yes, in the first Bill, in the second Bill and in the third Bill of which you spoke, **(Laughter)** *we are quite comfortable with them".*

Senator Keste Miller:
"You are speaking to all three, trinity".

Senator Anthony Johnson continued:-
"The man said all three so I have to speak to all three. It's what he says. I am not the Leader of Government Business, I have to follow what he says. So we don't have any problem with it. The Opposition supports it". **(Applause)**

Senator the Honourable Minister Deika Morrison had this to say:-
"Madam President, notwithstanding the discussion about by-elections and certain constituencies, etcetera, the Bills before us really don't speak to the procedure for calling an election or any particular constituency.

So I would really hope that as the debate goes on we can stick to what is contained here, because it is not an insignificant amendment.

In every country in the world people have died, people have died giving their lives so that people like me, a woman, a woman of colour can have the right to vote and I think that it is ...(Sotto voce comments)

I think that it is very important that we are moving towards ... **(Sotto voce comments)** *I think it's very important that we are moving towards better means of identification. But technology is not infallible, as we know.*

I'm very pleased with this amendment because it calls for, in the event of a failure that you have to take an oath as to your identity; and I think that's very important. I just want to give my support to the Bills. Thank you". **(Applause)**

Senator A.J. Nicholson, the Honourable Attorney-General had this to say:-

Madam President, these three little Bills hold the profoundest significance for a number of issues related to our societal arrangements. These three little Bills.

First, they address what I consider, and which I hope we all consider , the heart of our democratic practices in Jamaica. **(Applause)**

Second, they speak to how we wish to define ourselves as a people, our maturity and how we wish to have interaction with and to live with each other in our country.

Thirdly, and perhaps most importantly, they demonstrate and represent the heights to which we can aspire and reach if we decide to do things together and if we have the will to do things ourselves.

I notice that there are certain persons in the society nowadays who seek to excoriate others who speak to us doing things for ourselves. Well, I have no apology about that".

Senator Anthony Johnson:-

"I didn't get that one."

Senator the Honourable Burchell Whiteman:-

"He means as a nation".

Senator the Honourable A. J. Nicholson continued:-

As a nation, as a country, as a country. Madam President, in 1944 the Representation of the People Act was introduced and it was declared that there should be the entitlement given to every qualified person to do two things, to do two things. One, or to be able to do two things. One is to be registered as an elector in the polling division in which he or she is ordinarily a resident; '44.

Senator Dwight Nelson:-

"(Inaudible comment) ... *six years".*

Senator the Honourable A. J. Nicholson continued: -

"And the second - you weren't born yet. Youth man. I thought it was even more than that late.

And secondly, Ma'am, to be able to vote at an election of a Member of the House of Representatives for any constituency if his or her name appears on the official list for a polling division comprised in each constituency. These two things.

Now this was the first time that this was happening in our country and similar provisions existed in the Kingston and St. Andrew Corporation Act and the Parish Councils' Act with regard to the election of members to the Council or to Council of the KSAC or to a Parish Council.

As has been said an electoral process which ensures one man, one vote, etcetera, as Senator Johnson has spoken to, that even before the 90s that, as he has said, has been the principle that we had hoped would guide our movement forward.

For over three decades, 1947 to 1979, our electoral system was plagued by ineffectiveness in its administration and, secondly, widespread malpractices. Now these couldn't have been allowed to continue. If we were to grow up as a people, If we wish to define ourselves as persons, as a country, as a society moving to become... **(Soto voce comment made by Senator)** *Not only civil, a civilized society, we could not have allowed that to continue.*

For thirty-two years, Ma'am, there were quarrels and disagreements between the two major political parties as to the way forward. I mean some of us who are young in the Senate, like Senator Morrison and Senator Morris and myself.... **(Laughter) (Soto voce comment made by a Senator)**

All right Senator Morris and Senator Morrison. Those of us in the Senate who are young or those of us in public life who are young..."

Senator Arthur Williams:-

"How about Senator Spencer?"

Senator the Honourable A. J. Nicholson continued:-

"Kern, oh yes certainly. Kern and you too, you know. **(Laughter)** *But Senator Arthur Williams, we have always said that we will age but we will never get old".*

Senator Dwight Nelson:-

"Like fine wine".

Senator the Honourable A. J. Nicholson continued :-

"Yes. But they should be told, and it is our duty and responsibility to let them know what used to happen. For thirty-two years the too-ing and fro-ing in this country with quarrels and disagreements . Senator Johnson said that we have come a far way. But it has been a rocky and sometimes perilous road. We could easily have fallen over the brink easily. Lest we forget.

The Leader of the Senate did not wish, and neither do I, wish to go into any specific instances and into any detail, but we must remember the outcry of the Jamaica Labour Party Opposition in 1959, after the 1959 elections.

*An outcry and remember the outcry of the PNP Opposition after the 1967 elections.
I am not going to say which was worse than the other, but there was the outcry".*

Senator Dwight Nelson:-

"1959".

Senator the Honourable A. J. Nicholson continued :-

"Whatever you want to say, But there was an outcry. **(Soto voce comment
made by Senator Johnson)**

*So them say, so them say. But he was not running towards, he was running away.
That's the difference.*

*So ma'am, steps had to be taken to put an end to things like bogus voting and other
electoral malpractices, such as gerrymandering and the like. Steps had to be taken.*

*Well August 17, 1979 was the date on which the Senate gave its unanimous support
to what was called the" "Electoral Reform Bill". And you remember, Ma'am,that that still
remains on the statute books as an interim Bill. Because the intention was, and is, that that
Bill, that Act should fade away when we have a new Act that would be entrenched in our
Constitution, as the Leader of Government Business has said. So it means then that after
that the Electoral Advisory Committee was created along with the Director of Elections,
who replaced what was called the "Chief Electoral Officer". I think in some parts of the
Caribbean they still call him the" Chief Electoral Officer". Ours is "Director of Elections".*

*And then after that no longer could the party in power influence the realignment of con-
stituency boundaries and the registration of voters. It couldn't happen after that. That was
the sole prerogative of the EAC working in tandem with the Electoral Office of Jamaica.
And we recall that the late Professor Gladstone Mills was the first chairman. I hope I am
right — the first chairman of the EAC, along with two other selected members ".*

Senator Keste Miller:-

"A blessed man."

Senator the Honourable A. J. Nicholson continued:-

*"Yes. Then the two major political parties each had two nominated members to the
committee and then the Director of Elections completed the eight members of the EAC. But
the Director of Elections didn't have anything like any casting vote or anything like that.*

*Now at the end of 1979 when the Bill was passed and was acclaimed by all well-
thinking Jamaicans, it was agreed that whichever party won the next general elections the*

EAC would be entrenched in the Constitution. Now we know that up to now that hasn't happened, so it is our duty to take this a step forward, step forward, to make sure that that piece of legislation, that institution becomes entrenched in our Constitution.

Now in the 1989 elections there was no outcry of bogus voting when the Government changed hands, but in 1993 the losing party was upset with the result and there was a report on electoral malpractices and it was circulated to all and sundry, condemning the winning party, alleging electoral fraud. You remember".

Senator Anthony Johnson:-
"Drafted it".

Senator the Honourable A. J. Nicholson continued :-
"You drafted it". **(Laughter)** *" You are the man. Now we know.*

Now Ma'am, the real date that we ought to remember is July 17, 1998. Because - remember what I said in the beginning Ma'am — these three Bills demonstrate and represent the heights to which we can aspire and reach if we decide to do things together.

There was what was called – established on July 17, 1998 -- the "Patterson / Seaga Accord ", which was brokered with the expressed purpose of putting in place an electoral system acceptable to all parties and bringing to an end the constant post election trauma that the country was subjected to, sometimes resulting in death and destruction , July 17, 1998.

And I am proud to stand here today and to extol the virtues of unity, because these three Bills tell us that what makes us the envy of many countries far and near, now that they have come about. No matter that there are wrinkles on the brows of some persons concerning what they call "the late holding of a by-election", no matter that, the important thing about these three Bills is that they have brought us to a position where we are the envy of countries far and near.(**Applause**)

And I have no problem in praising persons who have gone into the trenches to deal with matters such as this. Senator Ryan Peralto, you have mentioned him already, but I have to mention him too, because he is going to be remembered for this". (**Applause**) *"I am not saying that he alone was the person who developed these things.* (**Sotto voce comment by Senator Munroe**)

That is another matter. I can't deal with that. Don't bother with that. Ask Bruce. Don't bother with me with that. You don't bother with me with that, you leave me out of that, sir.

No sir.

I am not saying that he is the only person who worked on the development of the process, but we know that he struggled. He was here with us in the Senate, and almost everything, even if we were talking about agriculture, a Bill to deal with agriculture, he had to find a way of weaving into the debate something to do with the electoral system".

(Laughter)

Senator Arthur Williams:-

"Keep your focus"

Senator the Honourable A. J. Nicholson continued:-

"Yes. And you know, Ma'am, we have progressed because the General Elections of October 16, 2002 ,we did not have any quarrels thereafter, the KSAC and Parish Council Elections of June 19, 2003, we didn't have any quarrels thereafter, the by-elections in Bethel Town and Mount Industry we didn't have any quarrels thereafter. I mean there were one or two little suggestions but nothing to detain us of substance.

Now persons who never did experience elections in the 60s, 70s, and all that, and they come now and they see this smooth wicket..."

A Senator:-

"To play on".

A Senator:-

"Ready to bat".

Senator the Honourable A. J. Nicholson continued:-

"And even if you get bowled you don't quarrel because you know that the wicket is true, they don't understand where we coming from. So what we are doing today, we are being part of a process of going a further step, the next imperative along the way ,you know, in the process of electoral reform, electronic fingerprint identification.

I know, Madam President, that the system that we have developed up to now will stand the test of time".

A Senator:-

"Hear, hear".

Senator the Honourable A. J. Nicholson continued:-

"Of course, it takes persons to make a system work, and if we in Jamaica, we don't have the will, the energy, the desire to have our electoral process which, as I say, lies at the heart of our democratic arrangements, if we are not willing, if we don't have the will to make it work, even this could fall apart. But it is not likely to happen, because as I say, in any situation in Jamaica where the two political parties, the People's National Party and the Jamaica Labour Party ,where they desire together to make something happen, it is going to work, it is going to happen , it is going to work.

So what this is telling us is that we can choose a different path than we have travelled in matters other than this. If we could get this right we can get other things right. **(Soto voce comments made by a Senator)**

Well, you see that is the problem that is the problem. If we continue saying that Senator we are not going to start, not going to start.

And even though there has been collaboration between Government and Opposition on this, I am proud that it happened under this administration. **(Applause)** *No question about that. I am not only giving praise to the collaboration, it happened under this administration.*

And you know, Senator Nelson, I am willing to discuss this with you, there is no government in the history of this country that has been willing, that has stretched the hand as much as this government, none, none. Never happened, none". **(Applause by Government Senators)**

Senator Dwight Nelson:-

"That's a matter of opinion".

Senator the Honourable A. J. Nicholson continued:-

"Well, if you can find one to match it tell me. But, that is not what I am dwelling on today. Today what I wish to trumpet is, is the collaboration, the collaboration between Government and Opposition to address a matter without which, without which we couldn't even attempt to get into the realm of the civilized.(Sotto voce comments) **(Laughter)**

Senator Morrison, Ma'am, suggested that because persons on the other side had brought up the matter of — that they really shouldn't bother with it. But there is a little something here, Senator Morrison, which as a country we are going to have to address and I know that this has to be part of the discussions that will ensue with what is called the Vale Royal talk. In the law at the present moment, it is only when a person dies between Nomination Day and Election, the person who has been nominated and he dies, then there is a stipulation in the law as to when that election ought to be held, it's only there that that is addressed.

For me, and I believe for this administration, I think that the law as far as the holding of by-elections should be addressed. Let us get together and decide how much time is a reasonable time and deal with it, you know. But I am only suggesting it I am not saying that it must be so or anything I am suggesting it, let us think about it. We have come too far with our electoral arrangements to make anything that we can do, we ourselves can do to make that turn over the whole bucket. We should not do that.

So, Ma'am, I end where I started. **These three Bills bring to me, bring home to me and I hope to the Senate and the nation three things: they speak to the heart of our democratic principles and the democratic processes in our country. Secondly, they address how we wish to define ourselves as a people.**

Are we going to be seen as persons just running up and down the place when an election time comes and even after like headless chickens, running up and down the place killing each other, bogus vote, electoral malpractice as if we don't have any sense. We can do better than that and we have done better than that and it is going to improve.

And finally my main point, it demonstrates what we can do if we decide to work together on any single issue.

I support the Bills Ma'am, and I would ask that we think of the Bills in that light. True it is that there is an overhang, that some persons say that Bills might have been done earlier and whatever, but let us look at the bigger picture. The bigger picture is where we have arrived and what that arrival can teach us and where it can propel us to go.

Thank you, Ma'am, I support the Bills". **(Applause)**

Senator Professor Trevor Munroe made this contribution:-

"Madam President, I wish to join with colleagues in giving fulsome support to the three Bills before us and in so doing to really agree with the Leader of Government Business and the Leader of Opposition Business as to how far we have come and to suggest that we need to even make more concrete the distance that we have traveled in order to allow those who feel that we are really achieving little or nothing to have a better understanding of the step that we are taking today.

Madam President, the historical record will show that as recently as 1993, the Electoral Advisory Committee following on that election expressed what it called shock and here I quote: "at the intensity of violence and thuggery".

The church leaders after that Election of 1993 again spoke and here I quote: "of incidence of fraud and thuggery by both the PNP and the JLP". Most dangerous of all, in 1994 which is but ten years ago, the people of Jamaica themselves now began for the first time to really doubt whether elections were producing results reflecting their will.

A Stone Poll of that year, 1994, found that 44% of the electorate, almost half, felt that the elections were neither free nor fair. And that 44% included, the Stone Poll found, 25% of those who supported the victorious People's National Party. So that when we get to that point where almost half the people begin to doubt whether the election is producing a fair and accurate result, then we know that we are on the brink, we are on the brink.

1997 big improvement in terms of election thuggery and election violence. But one particular statistic very relevant to the three Bills before us, in two hundred and fourteen of the polling divisions, Madam President, two hundred and fourteen, of the six thousand two hundred and ninety four polling divisions, more than one hundred percent of the registered electorate voted; in other words, bogus to the point of over voting in two hundred and fourteen polling divisions.

And therefore when we come to these three Bills we have to acknowledge that these form a crucial element of pulling us back from that brink and, indeed, consolidating what in 2002 was now regarded as an exemplary electoral arrangement. In fact, it was the Carter Center who, after observing the 2002 Elections, said that the 2002 Jamaican elections were exemplary in its organization and preparations and reflected adequately the will of the people. So that in the space of ten years we pulled ourselves back from a brink on which we were tottering from the late 70s into the middle of the 90s and that is a remarkable achievement, Madam President, which not only needs to be acknowledged in general, but documented in its detail in the way that I have attempted.

Not only did we pull ourselves back from that brink of disaster, but as I believe the learned Attorney-General said, in that way we have become the envy of many states in the world, including the United States of America, which despite its much vaunted democratic procedures cannot claim in 2005 to have as mature, as developed electoral system and electoral administration as we have in Jamaica, and perhaps we should send observers to their election in order to demonstrate to them how elections need to be run as we have done in recent years.
(Applause)

This is not a matter to be taken for granted. It could have been otherwise.

The learned Attorney-General was very appropriate in that remark. And if you want to understand how it could have been otherwise, Madam President, we need only look at some of what happened in those countries, and there were six of them, which achieved Independence in the same year that Jamaica achieved Independence, 1962.

Because we started on an independent road then and so did they, but of those six countries we are the only one despite all the imperfections, despite all the blemishes, despite all the deformations that have avoided some of the disasters that have occurred. And I want to crave the indulgence of the Senate to simply identify those countries which went away in certain respects that we could have gone but did not go because at critical moments we as a people, political parties and civil society, were able to unite, to come together and say, no, we have to pull back.

Algeria, Independence 1962. Madam President, Algeria has had a civil war in which over one hundred and fifty thousand people have died.

Rwanda, Independence 1962, just like Jamaica, genocide and a coup resulted in hundreds of thousands of people being slaughtered.

Burundi, Independence, 1962, ethnic violence, the assassination of the President, in which two hundred and odd thousand people have died.

Uganda, Independence, 1962, two coups, 1971 and 1985, two hundred and fifty thousand opponents of President Obote killed.

Trinidad and Tobago, Independence 1962. In 1990, an attempted coup in which the Prime Minister and eight Members of Parliament, Ministers, were held hostage for four days, 23 people died. Independence.

Finally Western Samoa 1962, assassination of Government Ministers.

Madam President, I only indicate this record in order to say that while our democracy has had its severe limitations and while many have been correct to point out that we have a long way to go, let us not for one moment forget how far we have come and let us not for one moment forget that those who embarked on the road of independence in our same year have had quite contrary experiences, which we ourselves could have fallen prey to, were we not as careful as we have been. " **(Applause)**

In that context, Madam President, colleagues, it seems to me that one of the geniuses we may say, one of the strengths of the Jamaican character revealed over and over again in the historical process, is really to pull opportunity out of adversity, over and over again faced with great adversity.

Internal upheaval in 1938 and out of that adversity pioneering in 1944, the first black country in the entire world to achieve Adult Suffrage . Twenty years ahead of the United States which only got to Adult Suffrage in 1964/65, with the Black Voters Act which enfranchised black people.

Opportunity out of adversity. In that time as well we were pioneers, institutional innovators in the Executive Council, the only colony in the entire world where the Executive Council was no longer purely advisory but became the principal instrument of policy, the harbinger, the predecessor to the modern Cabinet.

And so jumping forward to 1979 and once again pulling opportunity out of adversity in those days, by coming up with the formula of the Electoral Advisory Committee.

A formula that many in the world are now looking at in order to copy because what it does is bring together political representatives with civil society in a manner that allows a unified approach to difficult issues.

And therefore, Madam President, I would simply wish to make some recommendations to that exemplary body, the EAC, recommendations very relevant to the matters we are discussing today. One of them Senator Golding has touched on, and that is the urgent need in Jamaica to develop a set of regulations dealing with campaign financing and political party funding. I want to agree with him and to remind us all that it was this very Senate in May 2002 on a Private Members Motion, which I moved at the time, which unanimously supported the need for there to be full public discussion leading to the development of some regime for regulating party finance in Jamaica and now is 2005, the urgency has increased and therefore the necessity for the EAC to look at these proposals is very important.

But I want to disagree with my friend in one regard that while the fixed election date is invariably an accompaniment of regulations dealing with political party finance and campaign finance, there are countries that have developed appropriate regulatory regimes in which that is not the case.

And I refer to the United Kingdom Parliamentary system such as our own, in which the Prime Minister still has the flexibility and the discretion to set the election date, but which from 2001 the United Kingdom, in their Political Parties Referendum and Elections Act, have produced a regime for regulating party finance which we would do well to examine and to look at. So while I am not disagreeing that that is normal mode, we shouldn't give the impression that unless we agreed on the fixed election date we would not be able to develop or to discuss and to look at models of appropriate party financing.

In the United Kingdom it is now required that every political party make quarterly returns and those quarterly returns are on the website of the Election Commission and in those quarterly returns it indicates who gives, how much is given and to which party. And you can go on the Election Commission website after this Senate hearing and you can see how much the Labour Party has gotten, how much the Conservative Party has gotten, who has given them how much.

It may well be Madam President that in the case of our parties there may be nothing to declare for a long period of time prior to elections.

But, nevertheless, I only mention this in order to indicate that disclosure provisions, which allow transparency to the electorate to know who is giving how much to whom, are part of their regime. In addition, of course, limits on election spending...

Limits on election spending is also part of their regime, limits on contributions and very importantly that part which might provoke most debate in Jamaica, subsidies in cash and kind to political parties in the conduct of their legitimate business.

So I want to agree with my colleague that this matter now has great urgency, both political parties have taken it on board and I would like to urge that the EAC, before the end of 2005, look at the recommendations, stimulate national debate and come up with some recommendations that can deal with this extremely important matter.

But in so doing, let me make a second recommendation, Madam President, to the EAC, and that is, before you begin to implement new law, before you begin to add amendments to the Representation of People Act, let us enforce what is already there."

(Applause)

"Let me say it again, let us enforce what is already there in order to generate public respect at a higher level; that those who make the law follow the law." **(Applause)**

"And there is a particular area which is shocking, which is scandalous that has not been enforced and it has to do with the existing requirements for election returns to be made by candidates within a specific time period.

To be concrete, Madam President, section 55 of the Representation of the People Act now requires that between the issuing of the writ for election and the holding of Elections a maximum expenditure by the candidate of $3 million is what the law stipulates.

Section 60 of the Representation of the People Act requires that election returns be made within six weeks on the form in the Act indicating how much was spent on what and, more importantly, from our point of view in this discussion, where the cash and kind contributions come from for the candidate.

Section 101(3) doesn't leave it up to the candidate to observe or not to observe, it provides penalties, penalties for breach of this requirement. And I had thought that perhaps that one reason why the law was not being enforced in this regard was that the penalties were indeed minimal. Not so, Madam President. Section 101(3) of the Representation of the People Act allows for those guilty of an offence of not making the returns, or making the returns in a manner fraudulent, that such persons be liable to a fine not less than $20,000 or more than $80,000, or to imprisonment for such term as the court may impose, being a term not less than three years.

And the court may, in addition to such fine or imprisonment, order that the election agent or candidate be disqualified from holding any post of election officer for a period not less than seven years from the date of conviction.

All I am saying, Madam President, if we have a law, let's enforce the law and of course, let us as well amend it in ways that make it more modern and up to date. If we were to enforce the law in October 2002 in response to questions I posed in this Senate, 79 candidates or agents made returns by the required date; 96 did not.

And there was a kind of all-party consensus in not making the returns. Because of the 96 who didn't make returns in accordance with the law, 25 were from the People's National Party. Not to be outdone, 30 were from the Jamaica Labour Party; not to be outdone, 25 were from the National Democratic Movement and six from the United People's Party. So there is a kind of general disrespect and disregard for this requirement of the law. And what I am saying, through you to the EAC, develop, please, an appropriate set of machinery to insist on respect for the law so that we who follow the law might lead by example and not just by precept.

And the final point, Madam President, I would like to make in recommendation to the EAC, this extraordinary institution that we have developed as part of our democratic infrastructure, I think the time has come to re-examine, to debate and to determine whether there is not a need to introduce an element of proportional representation into our electoral arrangements.

It is not a new idea, Madam President. Former Prime Minister, The Most Honourable Michael Manley, put forward that thought in the 1980s, the Duffus Commission of 1986 made a recommendation that it be seriously examined. Prime Minister P.J. Patterson in a 1995 presentation on Constitutional Reform made a proposal that an element of proportional representation be incorporated into our electoral administrative arrangement and the Private Sector Organization of Jamaica in the 90s as well made such a recommendation.

I do so now for two reasons, Madam. One, is the 'dis-proportionality' in representation over the years in Jamaica. What do I mean by this? That our electoral system, the first-past-the-post system, as it does in most other countries, produces a higher level of representation in the Parliament, in the House in terms of seats for the winning party than its proportion of support amongst the voters justifies. And conversely whoever loses the election gets less percentage seats than the percentage support amongst the population in that particular election. And I just want to make the point very concrete to understand why I say this.

The 1967 election, People's National Party lost that election and it got in losing, 49 percent of the votes but it got only 38 percent of the seats, under-representing the party by 11 percent in terms of the proportion of the population supportive of it. 1972 Jamaica Labour Party got 43 percent of the votes; 30 percent of the seats, under-representing the minority party again.1980, PNP in that election got 41 percent of the votes, 15 percent of the seats, under-representation by 26 percent.

The last election was, therefore, unusual in that the degree of under-representation was less than it had been in the past. The losing party then got 39 percent of the votes — sorry 47 percent of the votes and 43 percent of the seats. So that the gap had closed . But that in Jamaican circumstances and the first-past-the-post system is extremely unusual and we cannot rely on that in order to look to what are appropriate arrangements in the future.

So this is the first reason, Madam President, because I think that the under-representation of the minority party has serious implications for how well the machinery of

Parliament can function; for how many persons there are available to sit on various Select Committees and to do the work of the Parliament.

And, therefore, I urge that we look again at an element of proportionality, not a total proportional representation but mixing the system in the way that Prime Minister Patterson proposed in 1995 and in the way that has been found very, very useful in many countries now looking at reforming their system. New Zealand, for example, has a mixed system that has worked very well.

The second reason for which I advance this suggestion is that the electoral system that we have, for reasons that we can't go into now, grossly under-represents half of the population; grossly under-represents women in the elected House. And this is not a Jamaican phenomenon. All of those countries, in fact 13 of the 15 countries which have representation of women of 30 percent of the Parliament or more, which is the norm set internationally, have some element of proportional representation and this is not a matter to be idly dismissed, Madam President. It must be a matter of shame and concern to us in this democracy that we have never, since 1944, gone over 12 to 13 percent, never, of women in the House of Representatives.

A matter of concern and I would go further and say a matter of regret, a matter to be corrected.

And I, therefore, urge that the EAC take on board the need to look at our system to see whether we may not put in some degree of proportional representation in order to reduce the discrimination against the losing party and in order to ensure and facilitate that women are more substantially represented in the House of Representatives than has been the case so far.

So, Madam President, I strongly support the Bill before us. They carry us forward, strengthening our democratic foundations; reflecting our genius at making opportunity out of adversity; demonstrating our capacity to avoid what others have fallen into, over that abyss. But I also urge that we are not complacent and that we build the unity to carry forward long standing proposals, like the Charter of Rights. I am on that Joint Select Committee, Madam President, as it was and believe you me, it is a matter of the deepest regret and concern that we have not yet been able to pass that Charter of Rights, because we have substantial substantive agreement.

So let us use that unity to build on the democratic foundations and to strengthen the democratic institutions, to enforce the laws as they exist and to reform and amend them where appropriate, in ways that I have suggested.

May it please you, Madam President". **(Applause)**

Senator the Honourable Minister Noel Monteith had this to say:-

"Madam President, I guess they know that I won't be long. Thank you, Madam President Madam President, in supporting this Bill, these Bills, I would like to note...

I repeat, Madam President, that in supporting this Bill I would like to note that at one stage I thought that I consider it rather unfortunate that we had to go this route in that, it will be a very expensive venture.

It is going to be expensive to provide the required equipment, to get the fingerprints and to compare the fingerprints. I consider it unfortunate that we had to really go this route and the reasons that we had to go this route, because of our dishonesty as a people. And I am not saying that Jamaica is the only place because we have heard of dishonest people all over the world in election. **We have to go this route because of garrison constituencies where more people vote than there are names on the voters list, and where one elector votes more than once.**

Now, Madam President, I support this Bill in the interest of honesty. I support the Bill in the interest of justice. I support the Bill in the interest of one man, one vote, or I prefer to say one elector, one vote.

And one thing I note, Madam President, although I am the only one mentioning the cost that it will be to the nation but I am pleased, very pleased that nobody else mentioned the cost. And I am pleased in that it is saying to all of us that we are prepared to pay the cost in order to protect our democracy and our integrity. (Applause) I am very pleased about that. *So, Madam President, in supporting this expensive venture, it is my hope that the process will achieve the objectives or the main objective, one elector, one vote.*

Madam President, I noted this before and I notice that a few people, the Attorney-General, Senator Johnson, supported that we have noted that we have come a far way. **Having noted that we have come a far way and those people who have championed the cause, mention was made several times of our good friend Senator Peralto , still refer to him as Senator.**

I think what we really need to do, what we really need to do as a people, Madam President, we want to ensure that our young people don't really take all of these achievements for granted. I think it is very, very important that we educate our young people, in particular our students in the secondary and tertiary institutions about the road that we have travelled in these achievements.

I remember sometime ago I had discussions with students from universities and with students from some of our colleges and I was surprised to discover that there were so many students who did not even know what was meant by adult suffrage".

Senator Anthony Johnson:-

"They thought it was adult suffering".

Senator the Honourable Noel Monteith continued:-

"And therefore, Madam President, it is very important that the history be told to them. I don't want to hear people talk about, well you have to put it in the curriculum in schools, because not everything you can put in a curriculum. But all our educational institutions, they have the leeway to bring in these things so that they can inform students. It is very important that they do so because what is most important is that our youngsters know where we are coming from, and that they don't go back there".

Senator the Honourable A. J. Nicholson:-

"That's right".

Senator the Honourable Noel Monteith continued:-

"The important thing is that they should go forward. They should build on what we have achieved. So they must be able to build on the past and they should not really go back. And I really want to emphasize the point.

And I noted earlier, and I have no problem in repeating this because the Attorney General made mention to it, that I must commend this government for facilitating the progress in this direction.

I would also like to commend the Opposition because this is one venture in which I know that they have co-operated and have shown some commitment..."

Senator Prudence Kidd-Deans:-

"Pioneered".

Senator the Honourable Noel Monteith continued:-

"Well, not pioneered it, this is the government that has facilitated it. And so I want to end by repeating also, because I had noted it to say and I have no problem in doing this,

that the electoral system clearly demonstrates what can be achieved when Government and Opposition work together for the good of the country. And so, once again it is my fervent hope that the objectives of these Bills will be achieved.

May it please you, Madam President".

The President:-

"Senator Miller".

Senator Keste Miller:-

"May it please you. I yield to my friend".

Senator the Honourable Minister Floyd Morris had this to say:-

"Thank you very much my colleague, Senator Keste Miller and thank you very much, Madam President. I will be brief in my presentation.

I rise Madam President, as a post-independence baby, to make my contribution and support for this Bill, because oftentimes it has been referred to us as the post-independence babies in the Senate as to not understanding the route that we have travelled. Madam President, various presenters today expounded on the virtues of us achieving universal adult suffrage sixty years ago and unfortunately whilst we travelled that path, certain unfortunate incidents might have crept into the system over that period of time.

But there has been a steadfast and committed endeavour to ensure that those problems that emerged and developed in the system are corrected. And one of the things that I speak about is the tribal nature of our politics that has developed over a period of time and thank God that we are seeing a significant change to that, especially since the turn of the nineties.

Madam President, this voting mechanism that is being put in place will undoubtedly contribute to correcting that tribal nature of the politics that I speak about, because I am certain that both political parties in constituencies where citizens were not able to cast their vote because the same person, the same individual was not allowed to vote, I am certain that this system that we speak about will serve to correct that particular problem.

And I am very heartened with that because as legislators, as leaders of the Jamaican society, we have to make sure that we do our utmost to implement systems that will seek to correct and reduce the level of tribalism that exists within our society. And as a young member of the team, I am very supportive of the efforts and the initiatives to address and correct that particular problem.

Madam President, there is one other issue that I would want to speak to. And before I came here members of the disabled community of which I am a part, asked me what were the implications for this legislation on individuals who have a physical disability and were not able to issue a fingerprint.

I understand clearly that the system takes care of that. And I want to really commend all the parties who have been involved as to the level of sensitivity and certainly to the administration of which I am a part, the level of sensitivity that I have seen being displayed as it relates to individuals with disability and it is demonstrated in this particular instance.

But I want to go further, Madam President, and make a recommendation and an appeal. Because whilst efforts are being made to protect the democratic rights of people with disability, there are individuals who have been denied that right in terms of access to polling stations from time to time, because a wheelchair user might not be able to enter into polling stations. And I want to appeal to the Electoral Advisory Commission and to both political parties to put that on the agenda to make sure that polling stations right across the country are accessible to persons with disabilities. I think that these are individuals — you know, Madam President, I was saying to the members of the community that the disabled man and woman of 2005 is a totally different disabled person of 1944, 1962 and 1979. He or she is an independent, progressive individual, who want to preserve their own rights.
(Sotto voce comments)

Ah! And some of them — the deaf will be getting their right to drive soon. And so, Madam President, I want to put squarely on the agenda, for both political parties, the Electoral Advisory Commission to make sure that the polling stations across the island are more accessible to persons with disability.

And as I part, Madam President, I want to say that I look forward to — they spoke about by-elections that are coming — I look forward to going elsewhere to do my work as we ensure that all citizens have one vote and the same person giving the one vote in the respective constituency.

May it please you Madam President". **(Applause)**

Senator Norman Grant made this presentation:-

"Madam President, I will be very brief — but I will try hard to be. But the importance of these three Bills is of such that I would like to register my full support to such a

passage and certainly let the records so reflect.

Madam President, the passage of these Bills allows for electronic voter identification system. Let me say , Madam President, that I want to refer to this as a tremendous step in the process of development and transformation in the country and what I would call a deepening of the democratic process.

I am forced, Madam President, to look at the process of development quickly, those events that characterize our past, slavery, emancipation, adult suffrage, independence and now what we call a free Jamaica. Let us take a journey, Madam President, quickly through the past to see where we are coming from and to therefore ascertain what has led us all to this point, a journey down memory lane. **(Cross talk)** *Very brief. We'll get there very quickly. We're going to take some short roads".*

Opposition Senator:-

"The farmers have short roads?"

Senator Norman Grant continued:-

"Slavery, Madam President, took place long before the time of the African slave trade. However, the area of relevance for our Caribbean experience suggests that slavery started somewhere in and around the seventeenth to the nineteenth century, commencing with the Amerindians and culminating with the Africans".

Senator Bruce Golding:-

"Why don't you start with the Arawaks?". **(Cross talk)**

Senator Norman Grant continued:-

"This - no, you see my colleague is closing with the...I am happy I am able to provoke some thoughts. This type of slavery, Madam President, was a destructive system that was predicated on the ideal that men should be subjugated on the premise of either their racial makeup or their religious belief. **(Cross talk)**
Yes, thus they had no rights. They had no rights, especially no voting rights".

Senator Bruce Golding:-

"And I thought that I was taking latitude with the Bill".

Senator the Honourable Minister Delano Franklyn:-

"No, man". **(Laughter)**

Senator Norman Grant continued:-

"Emancipation, Madam President, is another walk down memory lane. This took place in 1838 and we all know what happened there. Adult suffrage another event.

Independence, we gained this in 1962 and all citizens were allowed, based on certain parameters, and encouraged to exercise their franchise.

I would like to say to my colleagues that it is quite obvious to see that we as a people have worked assiduously to know where we are coming from and to also work towards a brighter future.

Voting is an important right. The right to vote is an important right. Our valued right to choose must be held continuously in high esteem as well as we must protect that right. And I want to commend the Government, in consultation with the Opposition and the EAC, for what has been done because we see this move, the passage, the ability to move towards electronic voting identification as a means of protecting that right to vote.

I would like to rush down by saying that we do have some very thought-provoking issues, Madam President that could create problems as it relates to the building of a nation along the protection of this right.

The whole question of crime and violence and in particular the political violence that marred our distant past. And here is where I wish to conclude by saying, when we look at the reference we note that in 2002, 59 percent of the voting population turned out. And this was six percent less than the turn out in 1997. I feel that the more the Jamaican voters feel protected and feel happy that it's one man, one vote/one woman, one vote that in itself could lend itself to more Jamaicans participating in this important exercise, thus the importance of this system.

But in conclusion, I believe, Madam President, that it is important and I want to use this opportunity and to use this Chamber to call on our present leaders to ensure that we as a country, we as a people will never go back to our ugly past as it relates to political violence in this country.

And I say this against the background that I would also want our political leaders, even in their utterances to so restrain themselves to ensure that even if there is an event that takes place , that we conduct ourselves so carefully that there is no indication or no pointing to any political tension between any of the parties. Because I think that the new Jamaica, those of us that want to continue to participate in an harmonious environment, it is important that our political leaders, and I know my colleague on the other side is now in a position where he leads one of the major political parties that we do everything possible to distill, harmonize, work together even if it will mean that we ourselves may be affected in this process. I think in the interest of building the nation we would be remembered in a very, very long time".

Senator Bruce Golding:-

"When you finish come with me to Gregory Park and tell that to the two families".

Senator Norman Grant continued:-

"Madam President, may it please you".

Senator Keste Miller made the following contribution:-

"If it pleases you, Madam President, it is indeed a pleasure for me to make a presentation in this debate.

I would say, preliminary point, what a difference one week can make, what a difference. Not to rehash what happened last week but I would like to make the point that someone said earlier on in today's presentation as a side comment, that our actions will be undermining the basis of the EAC. I beg to differ.

Because while I can understand the bipartisan approach to matters having to do with EAC, and that is good, we in this House, we are a review Chamber and we cannot lose sight of that. We are here for a purpose and that is to review and I will not relinquish that as long as I am in this House. Because even when you believe a Bill is perfect there is something in it that may slip the eye.

So I will address certain aspects of the Bill as I go on. **But I make the point that from I was in primary school I have been hearing this word 'bogus voting', bogus voting, every election, bogus voting. And I asked my father, when I was a little child, "what they mean, daddy, by bogus voting?" Him sey, "When people vote inna yuh name and when yuh turn up to vote, yuh hear seh people vote inna yuh name."** *And he gave me some other examples.*

There was a time when elections were run on lists so outdated, we don't want to go there again.

So it is important because I would say, you know, Madam President and Members of this House, I don't know of any other event that generates so much passion in the Jamaican people like election, election, election. **Because it is important, whether it is internal party election or national elections or even election to appoint a chairman of a board, it is election, a man love vote. And that is why we want to defend the vote with our lives. Like how those have given their lives for us to get the vote. So this is serious business".**

Senator Arthur Williams:-
"You have two minutes".

Senator Keste Miller continued: -
"Serious business -- I can talk until next week but I am not going to take that liberty. I know today is one day when they will sit on that Side and listen because they want this Bill, we want the Bill too.

Madam President, I heard an earlier speaker speak about fixed election dates and I must say that while you can set parameters within which you will set your date, this thing of fixing election for a specific date is a terrible thing because one thing it does for sure, the minute you finish an election, another campaign start. That is dangerous.

It can happen in some countries where they have a lot of money and people are spread all over the place; small countries like these will have a problem with that because Government need time to settle down and work. I am not into this idea of fixing date. Stay within a parameter and work within that parameter. No fixing of date".

Senator Arthur Williams:-
"Hear, hear."

Senator Keste Miller continued: -
"Knock wood, man, knock wood. Say so.

Madam President, I would want to make the point that while this Bill is a good Bill there are so many other things we need to address in our political affairs.

My friend touched on one, the question of political violence. And I will touch another one which is prevalent in some constituencies, where voters have gone through the trouble of facing perilous times to get their names on the list, because the vote is important. But polling stations are placed in certain areas where if you don't support a certain side you can't go there to vote. These stations are situated in some places where you cannot go".

Senator Arthur Williams:-
"We soon fix that. Just pass the Bill."

Senator Keste Miller continued:-

"You will have your Bill. I will tell you, you will have your Bill. Even if it takes one person today to vote, you will have your Bill. I will speak, Madam President, on a precedent that was raised by my friend, Miss Lightbourne.

A precedent that happened some time ago having to do with the Lower House and a by-election, precedent. And I am saying it is in our democracy that the Opposition should always be in a position to take Government because they are the alternate Government. So politicians must always be on the ready when an election is called, you must be on the ready.

Now, there is that instant that they spoke about, but the question I would like to ask them, do they see that as a fitting precedent?

If they can't answer I will answer for them. It cannot be. It cannot be because on this occasion there was an understanding that certain things would come in place before you call an election. I don't know that these conditions had prevailed then.

I don't know but I don't think so. On that particular occasion there was no matter to come to a House of Representatives to deal with before you call that election.

So it is a bad precedent. And I ask the Members of the House to just disregard it. Not a good precedent".

Senator Arthur Williams:-

"You can sit down."

Senator Keste Miller continued:-

"Remember, the main presentation that I had for today I am going to bypass it because I am batting towards the end of the innings but if you want me to put up my batting skills, my friend, I will and draw from my main speech. But it is good to know that as a nation we are getting to that point where after an election we can look at the results and say hey, we are well beaten, and say congratulation to the winner, because the people have spoken".

Senator the Honourable Minister Deika Morrison:-

"That is right."

Senator Keste Miller continued:-

"Madam President, it is not a nice feeling when you walk into a polling station to vote and hear seh yuh vote already and you know you weren't there, which takes me to the point that I want to raise about this Bill. There is a point about the Bill I want to raise for us to ponder".

Senator Prudence Kidd-Deans:-
"Which one?".

Senator Keste Miller continued:-
"Allow me. On page 2 of - that is 3(b) sub-paragraph on the - I think all of them have it, Representation of the People Act."

Senator Arthur Williams:-
"All of them are the same".

Senator Keste Miller:-
"Yes. Where it speaks about: Where the elector refuses to place his finger in or on the specified...."

Senator Arthur Williams:-
"3c".

Senator Keste Miller continued:-
"It tells us what will happen when that failure takes place. The question I would like to ask is this. If John Brown should go into that polling station knowing very well he is going to present to the presiding officer that he is John Tom, he refuses to do certain things and certain consequences follow, it tells you what will happen that they will do some erasing lines and all these things. What is the counterbalance for when the right man comes and somebody's name – remember that name in the book, that name".

Senator Arthur Williams:-
"That's a different matter ". **(Inaudible comment)**

Senator Keste Miller:-
"I am making my own enquiries, so if you can answer them give me the answer".

Senator Arthur. Williams:-
"You have another 30 minutes to talk."

Senator Keste Miller continued:-
"I am making my own enquiries".

Senator Arthur Williams:-

"You have another 30 minutes" **(Sotto voce comments)**

Senator Keste Miller continued:-

"So that person leaves the station, a line is drawn through the name that is in the book and that man with the correct name comes forward to vote. What is going to happen? What is going to happen to that man, the real man who is now there? **(Sotto voce comments)** *Because somebody is going to say to him, hey your name has been struck".*

Senator Dorothy Lightbourne:-

"It goes through the process ..."

Senator Keste Miller continued:-

"Ah! Someone says it goes through the process. Is that your opinion or it's a matter of law? It's a matter of fact? Are you providing the answer ?".
(Sotto voce comments)

Senator Bruce Golding:-

"What happens now".

Senator Keste Miller continued:-

"You see one of the things that we must think about, one of the things we must think about, there are a lot of people out there who from time to time have been frustrated in their efforts to poll their vote. If you want call it garrison, call it garrison. Find a name for it, but people are frustrated".

Senator Arthur Williams: -

"What's the point? What's the point?".

Senator Keste Miller continued:-

"The point is that we are going to pass a Bill today. **(Sotto voce comments)** *We are going to pass a Bill today".*

Senator the Honourable Deika Morrison:-

"Three".

Senator the Honourable Delano Franklyn:-

"Three, three, three."

Senator Keste Miller continued:-

"Yes not only one, not only two but three".

Senator Arthur Williams:-

"You don't know. How you know we're going to pass three?".

Senator the Honourable A. J. Nicholson:-

"Divide".

Senator Keste Miller continued:-

Because they will ensure that we pass it. They want it to be passed. Those on the other side, I say. They want it to be passed. But these are very pivotal issues for which I want answers". **(Laughter) (Sotto voce comments)**

"Don't ask me to ask the Leader ..."

Senator Bruce Golding:-

"Are you proposing an amendment?

Senator Keste Miller continued :-

You want an amendment? If you want one say so. If you want one say so. We can ask for an adjournment for us to get the opinion of the EOJ. We can ask now for a suspension ..."

Senator the Honourable A. J. Nicholson:-

"Move that the House be adjourned". **(Laughter)**

Senator Keste Miller continued:-

"We can ask for a suspension and ask that representatives of the EAC come and help us through this one. Do you want us to do that? Do you want us to do that?" **(Sotto voce comments)**

Senator Arthur Williams:-

"Ask if they are in agreement. Let's get their agreement".

Senator Keste Miller continued:-

"Programme, you know ". **(Laughter)** **(Sotto voce comments)**

Senator the Honourable Delano Franklyn:-

"Oh, no, no there is no problem over here, absolutely none".

Senator Keste Miller continued:-

"You know, this is how the political mind works. Last week I kept asking a question because I didn't know the answer. I kept asking, why do you want the Bill to debate last week and I kept asking, genuinely did not know what was the reason until somebody relented and said, oh, it has to do with a by-election. By-election, by-election? These are matters of principle.".

Senator Bruce Golding:-

"As a matter of fact we should refer it to a select committee".

Senator Keste Miller continued:-

"So now ... **(Laughter/Applause)** **(Sotto voce comments)**
Do you want us to put that to the vote? Do you want us to put that to the vote? I may just invite, Madam President to ask the question".

Senator the Honourable A.J. Nicholson:-

"Put it to the vote."

Senator Arthur Williams:-

"You want to return the favour". **(Sotto voce comments)**

Senator:-

"Put it to the vote".

Senator Keste Miller continued:-

"I have all the time in the world to wait. I have all the time to wait. I have up until 2007 to wait. I can wait until 2007. I can wait until 2007."

Senator Bruce Golding: -

"I think we should tell the EAC that they don't know what they are doing".

Senator Keste Miller continued:-

"How could we ever tell the EAC that? But what you must remember, the EAC can only send things to us to consider, they can't pass it. We have to deliberate and pass it. And we have a right to ask questions and we will ask them".

Senator the Honourable Delano Franklyn:-

"Move the motion, Bruce. Bruce, move the motion". **(Sotto voce comments)**

Senator Keste Miller:-

"So, Madam President, it is, it is my, it is my view that this is a Bill, this is a Bill which is well timed. It is a Bill that touches at the very heart of our democracy.

And I'm asking my friends on the other side. I'm asking my friends on the other side to show their support by voting for this Bill. **(Applause)** *Voting for this Bill , voting for this Bill. We want to see them vote when the question is put. Those are my comments. May it please you".* **(Applause)**

Senator Bruce Golding:-

"You need a cup of fish tea". **(Laughter)**

Senator the Honourable Burchell Whiteman then wound up this debate:-

"Madam President, there are a number of issues raised today and I will not attempt to address all of them. Because you see, unlike my colleague Senator Johnson who deliberated on matters which were only tenuously connected with the Bill, I am going to focus on the matters relating directly to the Bill and, therefore, I will be brief.

But I just want to make one preliminary point that, just to say, again I think the public needs to know this. These Bills were not dreamt up and brought to the Parliament after the middle of January.

They have been in the pipeline since, I think it was early September, August, late August return, to early September; and so it is not a case of something suddenly being created for a particular purpose which became necessary after that time.

Let me take my colleague Senator Miller out of his misery. I know that ... **(Laughter)** *I want to assure you, I have it on good authority, my colleague Senator Miller that the Opposition is going to vote for these Bills. They are going to support them, there will be no divide.* **(Inaudible comment)**

Oh, really? Okay". **(Laughter)**

In respect of **(Inaudible comment)** *In respect of.. No there will be no divide, I'm sure of this one. In respect of the provision for the person where an impersonation has been* *attempted, that person is protected, that person will be able to vote once that person properly identifies himself either by the fingerprint method or some other. Because the issue here is because this is now the method of voting if you choose not to vote, if you choose not to adopt the method of voting then you will not vote. You fingerprint yourself or where the system breaks down then you have an alternative.*

If you choose not to use the finger printing method or if you are not disabled and therefore have to find another method of identifying yourself then you have lost the right to vote. But the person who is the elector, the genuine elector who wishes to vote will come and be allowed to vote. Not be disfranchised".

Senator Arthur Williams:-
"Argument done"

Senator the Honourable Burchell Whiteman continued:-
"Couple of other points Madam President".

Senator the Honourable A. J. Nicholson:-
"Is the first I ever see so much sweat". **(Laughter)** *"Arthur is sweating, Arthur is sweating".* **(Sotto voce comments)**

Senator:-
"What happen to Arthur today?"

Senator the Honourable Burchell Whiteman continued:-
"I want to address - because we are focused .. (Sotto voce comments)

Madam President, much of the debate on both sides has focused on improvements to the system, the strengthening of our democracy and the fact that we are coming together as a people to do what is right for the people and for the sustaining of our civilization.

Now, Senator Morris made a very important point. However, while it is desirable that we should get to the point where every polling station where people are going to vote should make provision by ramps and otherwise for wheel chair patients to preserve their independence because they can, of course be assisted in other ways but to preserve their sense of independence, the reality is that many of our premises now do not have those facilities.

Many of them are private premises, they are peoples' private premises and, therefore, we can't guarantee - I know some provision could be made but you can't ask a person to do that and insist that they do if you are using their private premises temporarily. Temporarily ramps can be provided, yes, and where that is possible we certainly would do".

Senator Anthony Johnson:-

"For the last ten or so years the EAC has as a matter of policy attempted to use public buildings. Indeed for the last four elections they have been mandated to use public buildings and private facilities are only used where a public building can't be found".

Senator the Honourable Burchell Whiteman continued:-

"Yes, that is a point but I'm simply saying the point and an answer has been given. The temporary ramps can be created and I know some places where that is done but at some time even at some expense and some difficulty because it involves more than just putting up something temporary.

However, the general point is taken, Madam President, but I just wanted to indicate that this is not, opposed but I wouldn't make any guarantees on it at this point. It is something we must work towards.

And finally two things. Finally, two quick points, the financing of the process of electoral reform has not been easy. And I think that when people make light of the fact that the Government has facilitated the process they forget that it has come at a cost. And while we cry out for roads and schools and other facilities we must not take lightly the fact that we have invested in this almost at whatever it is that the EAC says we should do we do, because we want to ensure that this most precious right of ours, the right to choose, is preserved and protected.

And if I may come to the very last point, the nitty-gritty of what Senator Miller had to say about location of polling stations.

A lot has been done in the last few years to ensure that there is some level of - well there is agreement about where the polling stations are located and that where they are located is - No, no, I know what Senator Clarke is saying - that where they are located arrangements are made that everybody can have access.

And I'm not now talking about the wheelchair people, I'm talking about everybody. Because there are enclaves where people feel uncomfortable to go and what the EAC has done, with the support of the security forces, is to designate certain areas as special locations, special centres and try to get very special attention paid to them in respect of the security.

And that of course is something that we within the EAC want to insist upon because we really believe that if you go to all this expense and trouble to facilitate a system of free and fair elections we should do everything we can also to make them free from fear.

And so it is our expectation, Madam President, that as we seek to implement this part of the system all the other elements will come together to ensure that people will be able to go where they need to go to cast their ballot on election day, whenever that is.

Madam President, I want to thank my colleagues for their presentations and to move now for second reading of the Bill".

(At 1:20 p.m. the President indicates the time and a motion is moved by Mr. Whiteman for an extension before recessing for lunch to complete the business of the day.")

The Honourable President:-
"The question is that the time be extended so that we may complete the business of the day.

(Motion put to the Senate and agreed to.)
"The question is that the three Bills be read a second time".

(Motion put to the Senate and agreed to.)
"A Bill entitled: **"AN ACT to Amend the Representation of the People Act"** *read a second time.*

A Bill entitled: **"AN ACT to Amend the Kingston and St. Andrew Corporation Act"** *read a second time.*

And a Bill entitled: **"AN ACT to Amend the Parish Councils Act"** *read a second time".*

The Bills were taken through all stages and passed by unanimous vote.

Chapter Thirteen

AFTERWARDS

I attended the debates in the Jamaican Parliament during March 2005 on the three Bills, generated by the Electoral Advisory Committee report of 30 August 2004, and advocated permission to use the Electronic Voter Identification and Ballot Issuing System in Jamaican elections. The statements made are quoted primarily because some members took the opportunity to record their knowledge of the abuses that have been a plague on the electoral system for over half a century. They should indeed know of this, having been involved in Jamaican national politics for many years, and some had personal experience of the facts of this history of abuses.

Some members in positions of senior party leadership did not think it important to address the substance of those Bills. I have, therefore, formed an opinion about the future of the Jamaican voting system. I am once again unsure if the critically needed reform of the voting process will ever take place. In my twenty-five years in active politics in Jamaica, I have seen how things get manipulated, and oh ever so often primarily purely for political advantage.

It is very instructive to note which members who are still directly involved in Jamaican representative politics debated the substance of those Bills, and expressed a desire not only for change but to support action to prevent such things from continuing to happen, and which members did not.

I hope that all persons who take the time to carefully read this book, will agree with me that it is very important to deal decisively and expeditiously with the problems outlined in this chronicle.

My fellow Jamaicans who do so will I hope decide, while they are still able to peacefully agitate for change, to insist that the system to prevent these malpractices be implemented as a matter of urgency. We now know precisely how to go about protecting our voting system against abuse by those persons who have no respect or regard for the rights and the wishes of the rest of us.

In their final years in office, the Most Honourable Edward Philip George Seaga PC, ON, and the Most Honourable Percival Noel James Patterson, QC, PC, ON, agreed on the importance of implementing the electronic reform of our voting system. Had this system been established before they demitted national office, I am confident that our nation would have been positioned to be spared the shame, and the pain, which I anticipate that as residents we shall continue to endure, for as long as the existing system is in place.

The history of Jamaica on the previous occasion when the country experienced a double whammy in leadership change in the political parties over a relatively short span of time, does not inspire me with confidence in our ability to sustain and maintain both political and social stability in the immediate future. Instead it evokes memories of the intense social instability of the 1970s.

Within very few months, the Patterson/Seaga Accord of 1999 is likely to be of questionable relevance to the delivery of good governance, under the new dispensation that has descended on Jamaica, and this despite the obligation that all political leadership inherently carries to provide responsible caring governance.

It is indeed regrettable and a real pity that these leaders, who like me were forged by the crucible of colonialism to independence, could not have seen to the implementation of the new system and so establish a fair method by which we would elect our political leaders in the future. They were in at the beginning of the effort to reform the process, if only they could have seen that the task was completed before retiring.

The new leaders of the two main parties have been involved in the political system of Jamaica for well over thirty years. The mantle of Prime Minister and Leader of the Opposition has now fallen on them. I fear that they may be persuaded by advisors who seek to establish a binding relationship, that it is both critical and urgent for them to take action aimed at displaying authority and establishing political dominance in the public's eye, regardless of the financial or social cost to our nation.

I am deeply concerned about this, as the effort of the new leadership cadre to consolidate their positions, may take pride of place over all other considerations for some considerable time. If as I fear this happens, it may serve to accomplish the objective of inflating and soothing the egos of a few, but it will in the process definitely increase social tension, and further delay the struggle, of the majority of our people for a better quality of life.

Jamaica cannot afford for a second time in 30 years to expend the precious energy that will be wasted to satisfy egos, especially in these challenging times. The passion with which so many individuals who are now in political leadership will pursue establishing dominance, in order to solidify their identity as National leaders, is I am afraid, going to be aggressively followed at the expense of providing good leadership. I note the way in which some persons are doing things directly or through others to solidify their position in their party hierarchy. It is very much in evidence. A similar callous approach may soon be applied to address national issues and is likely to continue to be pursued at the expense of providing good quality governance.

I am gravely concerned about the Jamaican Parliamentary Elections which are due in 2007. The impetus that existed over some three years up to early 2005 to install the "Electronic Voter Identification and Ballot Issuing system" islandwide is no longer in evidence. The curtain seems to have been drawn on the reform of the voting process and this important reform appears to have fallen off the national agenda.

We have again begun to hear of some highly placed party officials, whose only interest is to win the next election, questioning the effectiveness of the **EVIBIS** and seeking to blame Abe Dabdoub and I, who were the last team from that party who pressed for its implementation, as not serving the best interest of the party. **I am pleased to note that we have not, as yet, been accused of not acting in the best interest of the Nation.**

I remain convinced that what is in the best interest of the people and by extension the country must always be treated, by those offering themselves for public office, as also being in the best interest of any political party that seeks to govern a nation. This is not necessarily true in the reverse.

If this system is not used islandwide for the next elections, those persons who aspire to be among those elected to lead Jamaica, will be trying to win by any means and at any cost, in an effort to entrench the new order. I, therefore, expect that Jamaican elections will return to the days of "lick down, tek wey " which may very well be in the interest of a political party, but will very definitely not be in the best interest of our people and our country Jamaica.

My children, who I sent to do tertiary studies abroad, had an arrangement with me to come back and help to build our country, but if after five years they felt uncomfortable living here or could not begin to make a success of their life, then they would be free to leave with my blessing to live in another country. Except for Aven and Jon who married Americans and decided to live there and Dia who died in a traffic accident there, my children returned to their homeland and tried to make a go of it as agreed.

As I write, five of them live abroad with fifteen of my nineteen lovely grandchildren. So does Velma my only living sister and my youngest brother Ronald, plus almost all my nieces and nephews and the vast majority of my cousins.

I became involved in politics to help preserve the land of my birth as a place where all my offspring, my wider family, my friends and all fellow Jamaicans could afford to live and would enjoy living.

I urge all who read this tale, to take very careful note of some of the fairly recent record of politically motivated national tragedies of our modern world history that are recounted in this book. Those countries are of a similar age of independence as Jamaica. They suffered those bad experiences primarily because too many of the people in those countries did not feel that their interest was being served by those who through manipulation got hold of, and controlled political power, and exercised governance.

If any Jamaican, after reading this book, has not seen sufficient reason to cause you to share my concern about the threat posed by the abuses of our system, of choosing political leaders to the future of our Democracy and of the country we call home, then I suggest you read it again. This time please examine very carefully the statements of our Jamaican Parliamentarians.

After reading this chronicle again and on closer examination of the facts made available to you, you just may decide as I did too many years ago that there really is a critical need to get directly involved, to make sure that the system used in your homeland to elect political leaders, is capable of ensuring, that only registered electors are allowed to vote and also ensures, "One man, One vote — Same man, Same vote".

Over the years, as I have sought to have this automated personalized system implemented in Jamaica, there have been times that I have had to draw strength from three teachings in particular from my childhood days.

1. **There is nothing a person decides to do that they cannot do, once they are prepared to spend the time and effort needed to accomplish it.**

2. **Be vigilant and be ever ready to stand up and defend your Rights**

3. **At all times have proper regard for the Rights of others.**

I hope I can get the support of my fellow Jamaicans in this struggle. I see a familiar scenario developing again. It is our off-spring who will pay an awful price in the future. We are obliged to make sure that proper steps are taken now to protect their right to vote to choose their leaders. If we fail to do so, they will I believe, experience a quality of life and governance that may be worse than that which some of our neighbours and friends have experienced and are experiencing, and this some of us were and are able to see first hand.

A line from the **JAYCEES CREED, "Government should be of laws, rather than of men"**, stands out in my memory as being particularly applicable in addressing the problem which countries continue to experience with their voting process, although admittedly, currently on a very much reduced scale in Jamaica. I have, therefore, taken the liberty of transposing this principle of that line of the creed to electoral problems.

"Security of a Democratic Process of Voting should be entrusted to systems and machines to guarantee its integrity, rather than left to the discretion of men".

Tarn Andru my second son is still involved in politics. I hope that he succeeds, where so far I have not. **I am sorry Grandpa Saunders but as much as we tried my generation just has not gotten it right, up to now.**

I have had the opportunity to be invited to observe elections in a countries in South Africa, South America and the Caribbean, and witnessed some of the difficulties that they experience. In addition, I have read some reports of difficulties experienced in other nations on the globe including the most renowned practising democracy in our world of today, which is the reputation of our largest northern neighbour, who from time to time has had real difficulty to guarantee the right of individuals to vote and that all votes are properly taken into account, to ensure "one man, one vote — same man same vote".

All of us who live under a Democratic System of Government must clearly understand, and accept, that we have a responsibility in our own best interest to do everything in our power to protect and defend the core and foundation, on which a Democracy is built and on which it rests.

It must also be patently clear that the heart and soul of Democracy is cradled in the principle that those who are to be given the authority and responsibility to administer, and provide good governance, must be selected by the majority of those who live in the society, and have the legal right to vote, and so participate in choosing who they wish to empower to exercise authority in their name, and govern over all others who live in that society.

For us to fail to protect and defend this right is to forsake the responsibility passed on to us by our forebearers, and to betray our inheritance and perhaps to deprive future generations of our people of the opportunity to live and die, clothed in the dignity, the pride, and the self confidence that is automatically generated just from being able to enjoy the previlege of living as free men and women in a democratic society.

This clearly means that every single member of that society who is entitled, and wishes to participate, in selecting those who will be empowered to lead, and has taken the steps to establish their right as an elector to make that choice, should never be denied or prevented from being able to vote, to determine who shall represent them.

There are some of us in our democratic societies who choose to put their right to vote on sale as a shelf item, available to the highest bidder for a mess of pottage.

To such person I say take the time to really listen and try to understand the message being brought to you in song by perhaps the most famous international reggae artist the Honourable Nesta Marley OM of Jamaica affectionately

referred to as Bob Marley as he sings his "Redemption Song". In delivering this message to his generation Bob Marley put to music the words of a Jamaican National Hero the Honourable Marcus Mosiah Garvey as he tries to reach our minds and our souls with the words "emancipate yourself from mental slavery, none but ourselves can free our mind".

I ask you to think of the importance to you to have the freedom and the right to choose those who shall rule over you. I ask you to think hard on the fact that this right was won by your fore-fathers who earned this freedom with their blood, sweat, and tears and handed it over to you to enjoy. You dare not continue to surrender your right and by so doing continue to dishonour your ancestors and disrespect their special gift to you of the right to choose who shall lead you.

To all others who read this tale you may wish, while it is still possible to do so by peaceful means, to exert pressure to cause such a system to be put in place and used, to elect the persons you wish to provide governance in your country. Such an act would contribute to the preservation of democracy in the country in which you live and remember please, it usually takes time to get fundamental changes, especially to implement a personalized system.

I pray that Our Creator will continue to bless all our countries and those who live therein, especially my fellow Jamaicans.

Oh my Jamaica.
Land of my Birth ---- Land I Love.
"Ad Majorem Dei Gloriam".

RYAN GEORGE SAUNDERS PERALTO C.D.
May 25, 2006

About The Author

JCI Senator Ryan George Saunders Peralto Snr., CD, was born and raised in Kingston, Jamaica where he has lived all his life. However, he has travelled the entire island and to many countries of the world.

He has been involved in community development activities from his school days. He attended St. George's College where he was tutored mainly by Roman Catholic priests of the Order of the Society of Jesus and from which he graduated as Valedictorian of the class of 1949.

He is a life long believer in an obligation to help to build a strong and happy homeland. This led him to forsake his thriving business operations and become directly involved in the politics of his country for over 25 years. During that time, he served as General-Secretary and then Chairman of his political party and also in both houses of the Parliment of Jamaica, and was appointed Minister of State in the Ministry of National Security, and later transfered to the Ministry of Foreign Affairs, Trade and Industry with responsibility for trade and industry.

This involvement alerted him to the weaknesses of the Electoral System of his country and caused him to spend a great deal of his energy and time in an effort to prevent these abuses from recurring.

He treasures his family, friends and country, and never hesitates to protect and defend them without counting the cost.